Enhanced Publicatio

I0014112

Enhanced Publications

Linking Publications and Research Data in Digital
Repositories

Saskia Woutersen-Windhouwer, Renze Brandsma,
Peter Verhaar, Arjan Hogenaar, Maarten Hoogerwerf,
Paul Doorenbosch, Eugène Dürr, Jens Ludwig,
Birgit Schmidt, Barbara Sierman

(Edited by Marjan Vernooy-Gerritsen)

PART 1: **Enhanced Publications: State of the Art**
Saskia Woutersen-Windhouwer & Renze Brandsma

PART 2: **Object Models and Functionalities**
Peter Verhaar

PART 3: **Sample Datasets and Demonstrator**
Arjan Hogenaar, Maarten Hoogerwerf

PART 4: **Long-term Preservation of Enhanced
Publications**
*Paul Doorenbosch, Eugène Dürr, Barbara Sierman,
Jens Ludwig, Birgit Schmidt*

AMSTERDAM UNIVERSITY PRESS

Publisher: Amsterdam University Press, Amsterdam
Cover design: Maedium, Utrecht

ISBN 978 90 8964 188 5 / E-ISBN 978 90 4851 176 1
NUR 953

Contents

About the contributors

Authors

Renze Brandsma is Head Digital Production Centre of the University Library of the University of Amsterdam. The Digital Production Centre offers scientists and knowledge organisations support to create and make available electronic publications, databases and repositories. Renze was co-author in of *Report on Enhanced Publications - State-of-the-art*.

Paul Doorenbosch is Head Research & Development at the Koninklijke Bibliotheek (National Library) in The Hague, Netherlands. In the DRIVER II project he was governing the development of a demonstrator for the long-term preservation of Enhanced Publications and author and editor of the report on this.

Dr Ir Eugène Dürr has participated in DRIVER II on behalf of the 3TU Federation. This federation, formed by the three Dutch technical universities of Delft, Twente and Eindhoven, has started a data-centre for the sharing and long-term preservation of scientific technical measurements. With a background as assistant professor in Software Engineering and a PHD on *The Use of Object Oriented Specifications in Physics* (1994), he has been researching at the Delft University the long-term preservation of technical data sets and programs in various projects in the last 5 years.

Arjan Hogenaar, MSc has been involved in the information field since 1983. He has been a Biomedical Collection Developer. Presently he is interested in distributed information systems. Hogenaar works at the Royal Netherlands Academy of Arts and Sciences, in the Research Information Department. He is a project member of the ESCAPE project, one of the Enriched Publication projects of the SURFShare programme.

Maarten Hoogerwerf, MSc studied computer science at Delft University of Technology. He works at Data Archiving and Networked Services (DANS) as a project leader and consultant on projects concerning durable infrastructure. For the DRIVER II project he was responsible for building a demonstrator of Enhanced Publications and currently he is associated with several other projects on Enhanced Publications.

Jens Ludwig, MA, MLIS studied Philosophy, Computer Science and Library and Information Sciences. Since 2005 he works at the Göttingen State and University Library in a variety of projects on long-term preservation and research infrastructures. He currently leads the long-term preservation work package in the "WissGrid - Grid for Science" project.

Dr Birgit Schmidt has a background as a Mathematician and is an expert on Open Access publication models. She has worked on long term archiving of digital objects, economic issues of internet-based publishing, and supports the collaboration between DRIVER and the German network of OA repositories. She currently coordinates projects in the Electronic Publishing Division of the University of Götiingen, including the European project OAPEN (Open Access Publishing in European Networks), the information platform open-access.net and other national OA projects.

Barbara Sierman, MA, studied Dutch Literature and started her career in library automation at OCLC-PICA (Pica at that time) in 1979. After that she worked at several IT companies as a consultant. In 2005 she joined the Digital Preservation Department at the Koninklijke Bibliotheek (National Library of the Netherlands), presently holding the position of Digital Preservation Manager. She has written several articles on preservation topics and participates in (international) working groups and projects like Planets and DRIVER.

Peter Verhaar, MA studied English Literature and Book History at Leiden University and Computer Science at the Open University. He currently works as Senior Project Manager at Leiden University Library, mostly on open access publishing of research results, innovations in scholarly communication and digital access to cultural heritage. In addition, he works as a Research Assistant and Teacher at the MA Book and Digital Media Studies at Leiden University. In DRIVER II, Verhaar was responsible for the identification of the requirements to store and manage Enhanced Publications within the DRIVER infrastructure. The findings have been documented in a report entitled *Object Models and Functionalities*.

Saskia Woutersen-Windhouwer is specialist Electronic Publishing & Repository Manager at the University of Amsterdam, The Netherlands. Her main focus is on informing scientists about electronic publishing, copyright issues and improving the workflow of the repository and the CRIS. In 2008 she was involved in the DRIVER II project, and co-author of *Report on Enhanced Publications - State-of-the-art*. She also works at Netherlands Institute for Ecology (NIOO-KNAW), where she is setting up a system to archive scientific data for the researchers.

Editor

Dr Marjan Vernooy-Gerritsen is Programme Manager of SURFshare, the programme of the Section ICT and Research of SURF, the collaborative organisation for ICT in higher education and research. Previously she was Chief Information Officer (CIO) of Cito, the Dutch national institute for educational measurement. As a consultant she was responsible for a nationwide project on the implementation of ICT in Education in the Netherlands, and advised Ministries of Science and Education in the Netherlands, Mauritius, and Turkey on that topic. Marjan has a background in biochemistry and informatics.

About the DRIVER Studies

The primary objective of the EU funded project *Digital Repositories Infrastructure Vision for European Research*, DRIVER (FP6) and DRIVER II (FP7), was to create a cohesive, robust and flexible, pan-European infrastructure for digital repositories, offering sophisticated services and functionalities for researchers, administrators and the general public. DRIVER's vision was to build a Europe and worldwide Digital Repository infrastructure, which follows the principle of linking users to knowledge.

Today Digital Repositories contain a full spectrum of scholarly materials, from theses, technical reports and working papers to digitised text and image collections. Sometimes they even contain sets of primary research data. Digital repositories may be disciplinary or institutional. In the future, Europe-wide Digital Repository Infrastructure will be a virtual network of physically distributed and peripheral maintained repositories from all countries in Europe. By virtually integrating multiple repositories from many institutions in all European countries, the network will build up a critical mass of research materials, which can be disseminated and presented to the world as a powerful demonstration of research output in Europe. This contributes to innovation in a wide variety of sectors and communities. Within this virtual network, each repository will maintain its own identity and will be clearly marked with a label of the providing repository host.

With the end of the first stage of DRIVER in November 2007, the test bed system D-NET was delivered, producing a search portal with Open Access content from over 70 repositories. DRIVER II moved from a test bed to a production-quality infrastructure and expanded the geographical coverage of Digital Repositories included in it[1].

One of the objectives of DRIVER II was to build a Confederation to promote greater visibility and application of research output through global networks of Open Access digital repositories. This effort led to the launch of the new international organisation COAR, the Confederation of Open Access Repositories in October 2009.

---

[1] http://www.driver-community.eu

DRIVER II significantly broadened the horizon of the whole DRIVER endeavor on infrastructure operation and functionality innovation by state-of-the-art and future-direction studies. After positive appraisal in the mid term review these studies are combined to three reports in the series 'Trends in Research Information Management'[2].

The European Research Repository Landscape 2008 by Maurits van der Graaf is an update of a similar study in 2006. It shows an increasing number of respondents and a further diversification in the character of a repository. These may be institutional or thematically based, and as such non-institutional as well. The ongoing process of widespread and diversification urges coherent approach, as a basic feature of repositories is the retrievability of information that may be dispersed over them. Continued monitoring of developments will be necessary.

Enhanced Publications by Saskia Woutersen-Windhouwer, Renze Brandsma, Peter Verhaar, Arjan Hogenaar, Maarten Hoogerwerf, Paul Doorenbosch, and Eugène Dürr, Ludwig Jens, and Birgit Schmidt is a state-of-the-art overview of the structural elements of an Enhanced Publication, as well as publication models, interrelationship and repository issues. In-depth study is made of object models and functionalities. More practically, a sample is given of datasets together with a demonstrator-project. In the final section, this book deals with long-term preservation issues, linking to the developments of digital repositories that are studied in other books in this series.

Emerging Standards for Enhanced Publications and Repository Technology by Karen Van Godtsenhoven et al. serves as a technology watch on the rapidly evolving world of digital publication. It provides an up-to-date overview of technical issues, underlying the development of universally accessible publications, their elemental components and linked information. More specifically it deals with questions as how to bring together the communities of the Current Research Information Systems (CRIS) and the Common European Research Information Format (CERIF). Case studies like EGEE, DILIGENT and DRIVER are analyzed, as well as implementations in projects in Ireland, Denmark and The Netherlands. Interoperability is the keyword in this context and this book introduces to new standards and to concepts used in the design of envelopes and packages, overlays and feeds, embedding, publishing formats and Web services and service-oriented architecture.

---

[2] http://www.driver-repository.eu

Trends in Research Information Management

Developments in digital data management disclose opportunities never seen before in the world of scientific and scholarly publishing. Research is no longer condensed exclusively in the traditional printed format with its fixed identity as peer reviewed article, journal or book. By losing this traditional identity the single steps in the process of research are becoming accessible as elements that seek context in new relationships. This poses two basic questions for data management: when is an element relevant and what kind of relationship is to be managed.

Data management has inherent questions and problems: uniformity, accessibility, durability and efficiency, to name only a few. Accessibility of the components of the research process will give rise to new ways of collaboration in research. These developments will call for a new approach, Research Information Management.

This series of books are based on trend analyses, an inventory on the scientific repositories in Europe, and state-of-the-art studies in the EU funded DRIVER II project. They are the result of in-depth discussions, troubling with uncertainty about future evolvement, and struggling with the formulation of definitions in the continuously changing world of scholarly communication. Authors, advisors, and reviewers showed perseverance in getting around with the selection of valuable standards and promising developments. I wish to acknowledge all members of the DRIVER community for their contribution to this work.

Choosing the format of a book is a rather traditional starting point that seems appropriate now, as we are only at the beginning of developments. Of course, the content will be presented in other formats as well and naturally in Open Access. And the form of an enriched publication will be pursued, e.g. when theoretical concepts are presented in a mock up or a simulator, as is the case with the 'demonstrators'.

In our series, mixing the format of a book with Internet information occasionally results in pictures of moderate printing quality. We decided not to enhance this part of the publication, but rely on referral to the corresponding Internet site for those who want further reading.

The six DRIVER reports are the beginning of a series of international publications on Trends in Research Information Management (TRIM). The TRIM series will host a variety of publications, mostly offspring of ongoing activities and projects in which SURF participates, written by well-informed authors.

Dr Marjan Vernooy-Gerritsen, editor

Utrecht, September 2009

PART 1. Enhanced Publications, State of the Art

Saskia Woutersen-Windhouwer & Renze Brandsma

The authors would like to thank Thomas Place (Universiteit van Tilburg), Anneloes Degenaar and Henk Ellerman (Rijksuniversiteit Groningen), Barbara Sierman and Paul Doorenbosch (Koninklijke Bibliotheek), Rosemary Russell (UKOLN), Peter Verhaar (Universiteit Leiden), Marc van den Berg (Universiteit van Amsterdam) and Maurice Vanderfeesten (SURFfoundation) for carefully reviewing our manuscript and for providing us with their comments and suggestions. We especially would like to thank Rosemary Russell (UKOLN) for correcting the English in our manuscript.

1. Introduction

In the digital world of scholarly publishing online access is provided to articles, hyperlinked reference and supplementary data. Connection with social networking, e.g. blogs, relation with other materials, e.g. multimedia, and semantic context, e.g. XML, is not realised widely at present. Publications and related objects are processed separately as single objects and connections between them are not easy to find. As no relation between single objects is provided, it is difficult to find out whether related objects are available.

Meanwhile, the number of scholarly objects on the Internet is growing very quickly. Integration of all this scientific information by linkage is necessary to keep publishing efficient and to maintain control over the process. Therefore, publications should provide those links, resulting in 'Enhanced Publications'.

Seringhaus and Gerstein (2007) have proposed an information infrastructure for Enhanced Publications; it should:

- capture a broad range of data in digital format and facilitate database deposit alongside manuscript publication;
- index all full-text journal articles, associate keywords and identifiers with database records and link textbooks, laboratory websites and high-level commentary;
- provide multiple levels of peer review, community comment and annotation;
- make articles fully machine-readable providing intelligent markup and structured digital abstracts.

Such a network of information should be accessible through a single seamless portal.

The infrastructure of information is becoming a more prominent feature now and the focus of attention is shifting from the publication as a whole to the structure and pattern of linkage between elements. In an Enhanced Publication this link pattern should support and reflect the relation between the publication and all relevant objects like data, Web sites, commentaries. This pattern can become quite complex and goes beyond what can be captured in the linear or sequential structure of the traditional publication model.

This leads to the question whether the current infrastructure of repositories, based on OAI-PMH, XML, Dublin Core, DIDL, or DDI, is capable of handling the more complex patterns associated with Enhanced Publications. If not, how will this affect the design of a new infrastructure? Will it be necessary to set new rules for Enhanced Publications?

To answer these questions, an overview is given of the current status of Enhanced Publications. Models are reviewed that reflect and support relations between objects in the world of scholarly publishing. Finally, a short checklist for repositories with Enhanced Publications is provided.

More specifically the following items will be discussed:
- Structural elements of an Enhanced Publication
- Publication models
- Characteristic features of objects
- Relations
- Current repository projects
- Conclusions

2. Structural Elements of an Enhanced Publication

Summary

With a view to preservation the publisher of an Enhanced Publication should set up rules about the quality of the file, file types, and links which may be used. Both publishers and researchers should invest in enhancing publications. Software and several tools for publishers and repositories are available for adding comments to online publications. Some publishers enhance articles by tagging the data in the article. For tagging they use many standards and ontologies, which are all discipline-specific. It will be difficult to provide these services on a more general level.

2.1 Elements provided by the Author

According to Van de Sompel and Lagoze (2007) structural components of a publication are:

- Semantic type, e.g. article, simulation, video, data set, software;
- Media type, e.g. text, image, audio, video, mixed;
- Media format, e.g. PDF, XML, MP3;
- Network location, because different components are
- accessible by different repositories.

Electronic annexes with the article are a common option, e.g. Springer, Elsevier, and Blackwell. Typical examples are: data sets, simulations, software, annotations, movies, computer-enhanced images, audio clips, tools and databases. The content may as well be the outcome of research as part of the research process itself, e.g. surveys. Annexes may be referred to in the article itself, but this is not mandatory.

```
A few examples of supplementary materials can be viewed at the
following urls:

    Excel (data)
    http://dx.doi.org/10.1111/j.1365-2117.2007.00326.x  (record)
    http://www3.interscience.wiley.com/cgi-bin/fulltext/118541732/
    sm001.xls (data file)
    PDF (data)³
    http://dx.doi.org/10.1111/j.1365-2958.2006.05221.x  (record)
    http://www3.interscience.wiley.com/cgi-bin/fulltext/118630076/
    sm001.pdf (data file)
    Movies
    http://dpc.uba.uva.nl/ctz/vol71/nr01/art02
    Screenshot of several results
    http://www.elsevier.com/wps/find/authorsview.authors/multimedia
    _supplementary
```

Figure 1. Example of supplementary materials

'Instructions for authors' for supplemental materials as produced by some traditional publishers give some idea of what this means in practice[4].

Publishers' checklists usually require that:

- All supplementary material is produced with a legend stating what it is, what format it is, and where necessary how it was created;
- Colour images are provided in the RGB colour space;
- Physical dimensions of the artwork match the dimensions of the journal;
- Lettering used in the artwork does not vary too much in size;
- Recommended file naming conventions are used;
- If a native data set is supplied, the program and/or equipment used are mentioned; or with specialist software like Latex, the software and version number;
- Extra rules apply for delivery on disk.

Most publishers supply instructions for multimedia files with details on the file types to be used. The instruction pages show how to prepare supplementary materials for electronic submission and include information on common problems, suggestions on how to ensure the best results and image creation guides for popular applications. They also offer special guidelines for Windows and Macintosh platforms.

---

[3] We found some supplementary material that could have been published as raw data to be converted to PDF. This makes reuse of the data unnecessarily complicated.

[4] http://www.elsevier.com/artworkinstructions and
http://authorservices.wiley.com/bauthor/suppmat.asp

Accepted formats are TIFF, EPS or PDF, but publishers are also aware that a number of authors already submit their artwork in MS Office formats for convenience. They accept MS Office files Word, PowerPoint, and Excel, provided that they meet certain conditions. Elsevier guarantees that they will continue to support these submission types, now and in the future.

On media types, Van de Sompel writes that a unit of communication should not discriminate between media types, and that it should recognise the compound nature of what is being communicated. It should be possible to allow multiple heterogeneous data streams as a single communication unit; as well as to recognise references to previously communicated units as formal components of a new unit (Van de Sompel et al., 2004).

Links to all types of objects by an author on the Internet, like movies and data sets, can be easily made in scholarly publications. It is possible to link to all kinds of materials on institutional Web sites or in repositories, and to blogs, independent of the location. Stable URL's are not required and not checked. At this moment links to an article on a publisher's site can only be added when the publication is created: not after official publication.

2.2   Elements provided by Peer Review

Researchers have increasingly the opportunity to add information to a published article. The most famous example can be found at the Public Library of Science (Figure 1). PLoS ONE is an international, peer-reviewed, open-access, online journal. The pre-publication peer review of PLoS One concentrates on technical rather than subjective concerns. It may involve discussion with other members of the editorial board and/or the solicitation of formal reports from independent referees. If published, papers will be made available for community-based open peer review involving the addition of online notes, comments, and ratings. This requires that they offer researchers an easy way of adding annotations, starting a discussion on an article, adding trackbacks, e.g. to blogs (Figure 2) and ratings. Other PLoS journals use or will use the same model although they use higher, not only technical, peer review standards. PLoS uses the Topaz software platform for the infrastructure of their journals.

Figure 2. Screenshot of PLoS One

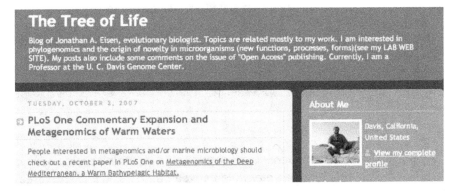

Figure 3. Screenshot of a blog concerning a PLoS article

Below some examples of other journals with open peer review are described.

Atmospheric Chemistry and Physics (ACP)

ACP is an interactive scientific journal with open peer review. It facilitates open peer review to show how other researchers have improved or enhanced a publication by their comments. Initial access peer review of ACP assures the basic scientific and technical quality of papers published. Subsequent interactive discussion and public commenting by referees, authors and other members of the scientific community is expected to enhance quality control for papers published in ACP beyond the limits of the traditional closed peer review.

Journal of Interactive Media in Education (JIME)

The open peer review process model of JIME shows three stages: preprint under private open peer review, preprint under public open peer review, and publication. This open model results in a more responsive and dynamic review. Reviewers are named and accountable for their comment. Their contribution is acknowledged. Thus, the research community has the opportunity of shaping a submission before final publication. Beyond this stage, discussions remain online, but cannot easily be referenced lacking a unique identifier or link. However, name of the author, email address, date and time are mentioned.

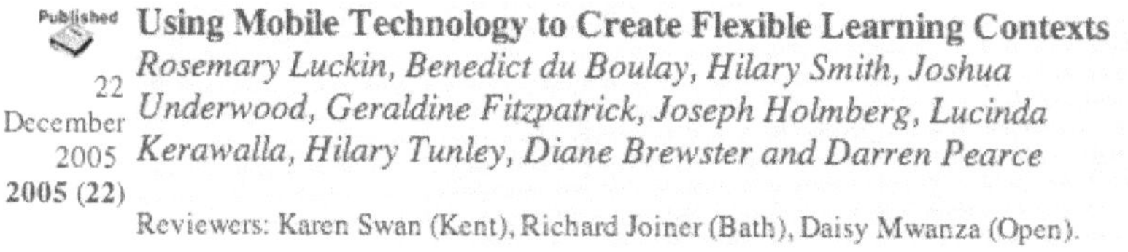

Published **Using Mobile Technology to Create Flexible Learning Contexts**
Rosemary Luckin, Benedict du Boulay, Hilary Smith, Joshua
22
December *Underwood, Geraldine Fitzpatrick, Joseph Holmberg, Lucinda*
2005 *Kerawalla, Hilary Tunley, Diane Brewster and Darren Pearce*
2005 (22)
Reviewers: Karen Swan (Kent), Richard Joiner (Bath), Daisy Mwanza (Open).

Figure 4. The names of reviewers are stated with the publication

JIME uses D3E (Digital Document Discourse Environment), a tool for document-centric discussion (http://d3e.sourceforge.net/). D3E easily transforms any HTML file into an interactive document that can be tightly integrated into topic-specific or section-specific discussion threads.

Economics

Economics adopts *"an open source approach to publication, viewing research as a cooperative enterprise between authors, editors, referees and readers"*. This approach is considered to be:
- *Quick*. As it uses a public peer review process, publication lag is radically reduced;
- *Democratic*. The quality of an article is decided not just by the editors and referees, but also by the community of registered readers;

Trends in Research Information Management

DRIVER studies (2006-2008)

The European Repository Landscape
Maurits van der Graaf & Kwame van Eijndhoven

A DRIVER's Guide to European Repositories
Rene van Horik, Wilma Mossink, Vanessa Proudman, Barbara Sierman, Alma Swan
(Edited by Kasja Weenink, Leo Waaijers & Karen Van Godtsenhoven)

Investigative Study of Standards for Digital Repositories and Related Services
Muriel Foulonneau & Francis André

DRIVER II studies (2008-2009)

The European Repository Landscape 2008
Inventory of Digital Repositories for Research Output in the EU
Maurits van der Graaf
(Edited by Marjan Vernooy-Gerritsen)

Enhanced Publications
Linking Publications and Research Data in Digital Repositories
Saskia Woutersen-Windhouwer, Renze Brandsma, Peter Verhaar, Arjan Hogenaar, Maarten Hoogerwerf, Paul Doorenbosch, Eugène Dürr, Jens Ludwig, Birgit Schmidt, Barbara Sierman
(Edited by Marjan Vernooy-Gerritsen)

Emerging Standards for Enhanced Publications and Repository Technology
Survey on Technology
Karen Van Godtsenhoven, Mikael Karstensen Elbæk, Gert Schmeltz Pedersen, Barbara Sierman, Magchiel Bijsterbosch, Patrick Hochstenbach, Rosemary Russell, Maurice Vanderfeesten
(Edited by Karen Van Godtsenhoven & Marjan Vernooy-Gerritsen)

- *Up-to-date*. Authors can upload revised versions of their publication in response to public peer review.

Registered readers may rate, recommend and comment and have the option to do so anonymously. Sometimes readers are invited to comment. Comments cannot be easily referenced however. They may have a name and have a date and time, but they are part of the publication.

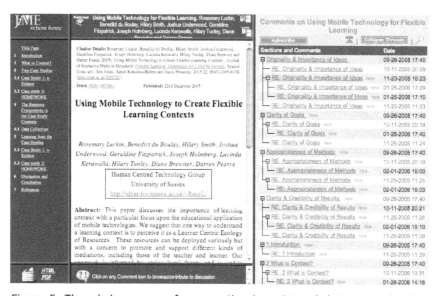

Figure 5. The whole process of commenting is registered, but cannot be cited easily

At the moment, none of the large publishers Elsevier, Springer, or Blackwell offer such post publication peer review. Nature only allows comments to news, not to publications. Some repositories provide the same opportunities for open peer review. In the UK, Richtags[5] facilitates cross-repository EPrints browsing and has an option to discuss and tag articles in the repository. The CERN Document Server[6] offers researchers the opportunity to write a review or a comment, and to rate a document. The National Science Digital Library (NSDL) allows insertion of a trackback in the repository when a link is created in a wiki or on a blog to an item in the repository.

---

[5] http://www.richtags.org
[6] http://cdsweb.cern.ch/

28

2.3   Elements provided by the Publisher

The most important role for a publisher is thought to be in enhancing articles, using XML and, in particular, a markup language for some specific areas of knowledge, e.g. Chemical Markup Language, Mathematics Markup Language and Biology Markup Language. Markup language assists in finding information and linking it to external sources. To enhance information in an article all relevant terms should be tagged. Relevant questions are: which are those terms, what standards are to be applied and who is responsible for the actual markup (Lynch, 2007).

The Royal Society of Chemistry has started an interesting project Prospect[7] in which publications are enhanced.

The following standards are used:
- *InChI* [8]. The International Chemical Identifier;
- *CML*. Chemical Markup Language;
- *GO Consortium* [9]. Controlled vocabulary to describe gene and gene product attributes in any organism;
- *Sequence Ontology* [10];
- *Open Biomedical Ontologies* [11];
- *IUPAC Gold Book* [12]. IUPAC Compendium of Chemical Terminology;
- *SMILES*. Simplified Molecular Input Line Entry Specification.

The publisher offers an Ontology Terms feature. If the article contains terms from the Gene Ontology, Sequence Ontology or Cell Ontology, drop-down boxes appear. Selecting a term opens a pop-up window, presenting further details and related articles.

---

[7] http://www.rsc.org/Publishing/Journals/ProjectProspect/ The Prospect View availability will be free or subscriber-only depending on the status of the other article formats (PDF and unenhanced HTML). The Examples page contains several examples that are freely available to all users. See also: http://www.rsc.org/Publishing/Journals/ProjectProspect/Features.asp
http://www.rsc.org/images/prospect11divx_tcm18-84747.avi

[8] http://old.iupac.org/inchi/

[9] http://www.geneontology.org/

[10] http://www.sequenceontology.org/

[11] http://www.obofoundry.org/

[12] http://goldbook.iupac.org/

Another feature is Highlight Terms. It offers three options, each of which will highlight different terms in the paper:

- *Show Gold Book.* Highlights in yellow the terms contained in the IUPAC Gold Book. Clicking on a highlighted term opens a pop-up window that links directly to the online IUPAC Gold Book.
- *Show Ontology Terms.* Highlights in blue terms from the three ontologies that may appear in the paper, the same terms that appear in the drop-down boxes, so the readers can judge the context. Clicking on a highlighted ontology term opens a new pop-up window providing a definition of the term, a link to online ontology and a listing of other related RSC papers that are enhanced and also contain that term.
- *Show Compounds.* Highlights in pink the compounds that are identified in the paper. Clicking on it will open a new pop-up window containing compound name, any synonyms, the InChI (IUPAC's Chemical Identifier), SMILES strings for the compound, a downloadable CML (Chemical Markup Language) file, and a 2-D graphic of the compound. A list of other RSC enhanced articles containing that compound is also available.

This enhanced functionality enables readers to judge the content of the article quickly, bringing up definitions and lists of related articles. The compound information identified allows for viewing and downloading standard information on each compound and provides links to other articles containing this compound. Downloaded CML may be viewed in the JMOL applet.

Some publishers use numbers or IDs from other databases, also external ones. Only a few of them have established active links, e.g. Nature linking to Genebank and the Protein Data Bank. Fink and Bourne are working with the Public Library of Science and a major biological database, the RCSB Protein Data Bank, to integrate the traditional concept of a publication and a separate data repository. They demonstrate that many publishers require the author to deposit the data of the publication in an appropriate public repository. On publishing a manuscript describing the structure of the macromolecule Macromolecular structure, data must be deposited in the Protein Data Bank. A reference to the publication is included as part of the deposition process. Unfortunately this requirement does not apply to further publications on the protein. They will link to the Protein Data Bank, but the bank itself does not contain information on these articles.

3.   Publication Models

Summary

After describing current models, we propose as a definition of an Enhanced Publication: a publication that is enhanced with research data, extra materials, post publication data, database records, e.g. the Protein Data Bank, and that has an object-based structure with explicit links between the objects. In this definition an object can be part of an article, a data set, an image, a movie, a comment, a module or a link to information in a database.

In every model it is tried to add a structure by using metadata on very different levels: module (Kircz), classes and instances (Van de Sompel) and concepts (Hunter, Marcondes). The aggregated object of all these models becomes more richly structured and exposes its semantics more explicitly. This structure is not only important for human reading and comprehension, but should also be machine-readable for data mining purposes. One of the difficulties is that adding metadata and/or rich structure is very time consuming. Almost all researchers mention the importance of creating tools to assist the author. Moreover (Lynch, 2007) mentions the importance of tools: "I hope that we will see a new generation of viewing and annotation tools deployed, presumably working on semantically rich XML document representations."

It appears that most metadata formats, like Dublin Core, MARC, and METS, are too limited for Enhanced Publications. The information that needs to be recorded cannot be mapped easily to a hierarchical XML structure. We are dealing with objects, properties and types of objects, and relationships between objects. To describe this intricate set of properties, we really need a graph structure instead of a tree structure. For this new infrastructure we will need to use the OAI-ORE model.

3.1   Introduction

Van der Poel (2007) has interviewed scientist about Enhanced Publications. He found three ways of enhancement:
- Research data, evidence of the research;
- Extra materials, to illustrate or to clarify;
- Post publication data, e.g. commentaries, ranking.

The practice of traditional publishers corresponds with the researchers' view of Enhanced Publications: short articles in print, and much additional material as supplements in online form only. These supplementary materials can be a valuable addition or they can make for a disjointed piece of work. In practice most of the supplementary material is ad hoc and cannot be readily queried across all articles (Bourne, 2005).

For the DRIVER II project we have searched for an alternative publication model that might help to structure all these objects into a logical unit, an Enhanced Publication. We have limited ourselves to Enhanced Publications, a "combined package of a textual resource and additional materials such as original data". It may be noted that publications that have no textual resource, e.g. data sets or movies, or movies demonstrating a protocol, are still rare, but are becoming increasingly important.

In the next two sections we will look at new publication models that have been developed to improve and enhance scientific articles:
• The modular article described by Kircz, and
• The semantic model by Hunter (Scientific Publication Packages) and Marcondes (scientific methodology structure in XML).

3.2   Modular Article

According to Kircz (1998; 2002) data sets, images, sounds, simulations and videos are part of the publishing environment, next to text. However, these objects should preferably not be simply added to the traditional article, which is described as linear. The better choice is linking them together into a modular article. This development into an article as an aggregation of independent but interacting objects or modules is made possible by Internet technology.

A modular article consists of modules and links between them into a coherent unit for the purpose of communication. A module is defined as a uniquely characterised, self-contained representation of a conceptual information unit, aimed at communicating that information (Harmsze, 2000). A module shows different forms, e.g. a data set in its basic form as a list of data, or conceived in a histogram. Each type of information unit should be well defined and therefore be endowed with different sets of metadata, each set describing a different aspect of the information entity (Kircz, 1998; 2002).

A modular structure allows for reuse of relevant modules that do not need to be rewritten for a new purpose. Well-informed readers may skip rereading them, depending on their wish to do so, their expertise or level of understanding. The modular structure brings more efficiency to both reading and publishing. The journal Cell uses a modular structure, be it in a somewhat primitive form. Older issues are freely accessible.

Proposed modules of a modular article are (Kircz, 1998):

1. Module meta information; the central module of an article
   a. Bibliographic information;
   b. Contents, revealing the structure of the article;
   c. Index terms, according to the relevant applicable standards of classification;
   d. Bibliographical references;
   e. Acknowledgments;
   f. Abstract.

2. Goal and setting
   a. The definition of the problem;
   b. The embedding of the research (methods, techniques, goals).

3. Results
   a. Raw data;
   b. Fitted data.

4. Discussion

5. Conclusions

3.3   Semantic Publication

Hunter (2006) introduces the 'Scientific Publication Package' (SPP) as a new information format that encapsulates raw data, derived products, algorithms, software, textual publications and associated contextual and provenance metadata. This new information format is fundamentally different from the traditional file-based formats. Hunter describes a high-level architecture that is currently under development. It enables scientists to capture, index, store, share, exchange, reuse, compare and integrate scientific results through SPPs.

The SPPs are based on an extension of the ABC model. The ABC model and the SPP are based on a number of scientific concept models for publishing scientific data and results, and for documenting the lineage of scientific theories and advances.

Hunter stresses the importance of workflow technologies as a component of the scientific process. SPPs capture the chain of processing steps used to generate scientific data and derived products, like publications. They also enable scientists to describe and carry out their experimental processes in a repeatable, verifiable and distributed way and to track the source of errors, anomalies and faulty processing (Van Horik, 2008).

At the end of the scientific discovery process, the scientist publishes his/her SPP, a complex, composite digital object encapsulating a variety of related heterogeneous components. These must be specified and can either be included as references to a unique identifier or actual bit streams incorporated within the package. Tools are provided to the scientist that allow him/her to specify the precise components, including:
• Data: database values, images, visualisations, graphs;
• Mathematical functions represented in MathML: input variables, output variables, constants, constraints;
• Software specifications: source code, executables, applets or links to Web services;
• Textual documents: EndNote files, notes, reports, documentation, annotations, publications.

The Scientific Publication Package (SPP) is then generated. It is a compound digital object represented as an RDF package. The relationships between the atomic objects within the compound object are either explicitly defined during the metadata capture, inferred from the rules associated with the ontology, or defined by the scientist during the SPP specification. Descriptive metadata for the SPP is entered and validated.

It is envisaged that this metadata set could be based on the extensible CCLRC scientific metadata model:

- Identifier;
- Title;
- Research focus/topic;
- Study;
- Model type, drawn from a hierarchical thesaurus;
- Creator/investigator – name and contact details, organisation;
- Date created;
- Date published.

The creator/author attaches a Science Commons License to the SPP. The SPP object now may be ingested and saved to a DSpace or Fedora digital library/institutional repository (Hunter, 2006).

Marcondes (2005) investigated the potential of 'Web published scientific articles', conceived not only as texts, but also as machine-readable knowledge bases, which are explicitly and formally related to a Web-based public ontology representing the assented knowledge of a specific domain. His goal is to enhance Web electronic publishing to embody new facilities provided by the Web environment in the semantic Web initiative context. As a first step towards this objective he has presented a model of an article's scientific methodology structure that has some elements in common with that of Hunter (2006). The methodology of Marcondes follows six steps:

1. Facts, or more precisely, problematic facts;
2. Formalisation of a research problem or question;
3. Development of a hypothesis which is an answer to the research problem;
4. Empirical testing of the hypothesis;
5. Analysis of the test result(s);
6. Conclusion: hypothesis ratification or refusal.

This methodology is a part of the proposed model. The model is an XML structure, hierarchically organised and mapped to XML elements, and has two types of relations, expressed as links: from an article's 'deep structure' to other articles cited in it and an available Web ontology.

```
<scientific_article_deep_structure>
      <fact>... </fact> ...                 (new phenomena)
      <problem> ... </problem>              (question)
      <method>
            <methodology> ... </methodology>
      </method>
      <hypotheses>                          (provisory answer)
          <contextual_condition> ... </contextual_condition> .
          <cause> ...
                <link to knowledge base> ...
                </link to knowledge base>
          </cause> ...
          <consequence> ...
                <link to knowledge base> ...
                </link to knowledge base>
          </consequence> ...
      </hypotheses>
      <result> ...  </result> ...   (data resulting of controlled
                                    experiences or empirically
                                    collected - also a link to data
                                    sets of results)
      <conclusion> ...
            (hypotheses ratification or refusal)
            <link to knowledge base> ... </link to knowledge base>
      </conclusion> ...
       <citation>
            <bibliographic_reference> ... </bibliographic_reference>
            <link to bibliographic reference> ...
            </link to bibliographic reference>
            <reason_to_cite> ... </reason_to_cite>
      </citation> ...
</scientific_article_ deep_structure>
```

All these elements are published as a 'knowledge base', using XML, thus outlining a Scientific methodology Markup Language (Sm-ML). Concepts expressed in the different parts of a scientific article are to be linked to public Web ontologies, thus enabling the establishment of a formal relationship between the scientific article specific knowledge base to ontologies like the UMLS – the Unified Medical Language System[13]. In Paragraph 2.3 we have mentioned the Prospect project, where Chemical Markup Language (CML) is used in journals of the Royal Society of Chemistry to link to ontologies.

Marcondes advises development of tools that permit:
1. Electronic publishing of research results both as text and as a knowledge base;
2. Explicit relation of this knowledge base to other scientific articles and to public Web ontologies, which store the established corpus of knowledge of a specific domain;

---

[13] http://www.nlm.nih.gov/pubs/factsheet/umls.html

3. Other researchers to navigate throughout a semantically rich network of enhanced text/ontologies articles, to check their validity and coherence, and to compare, comment and semantically query them.

According to Marcondes, the proposed model will improve the scientific communication process. With the aid of intelligent software agents the rich Web environment will permit browsing and navigation, semantic retrieval, critical enquiry, semantic citation, comparison, coherence verification and validating a scientific article against Web public ontologies. His model is also conceived as the basis for developing enhanced authoring and retrieval tools.

Fink and Bourne (2007) are developing authoring tools to make the use of XML significantly easier. In their project, they use the NLM DTD (National Library of Medicine - Document Type Definition) to store a publication in a standardised and machine-readable format. This DTD also includes some semantic markup of the content, unique identifiers for the article itself and for the objects, e.g. figures and tables, within it. The tool they are developing in the project BioLit is a set of open-source tools that will facilitate the integration of open literature and biological data. Initially, they will develop and test these tools using the entire corpus of the Public Library of Science (PLoS) and the Protein Data Bank (PDB). Although biological objects are being used, the aim is to design tools that will be generally applicable to all literature and other biological data.

3.4   Repository Interoperability

The essence of the open archives approach is to enable access to Web-accessible material through interoperable repositories for metadata sharing, publishing and archiving. The OAI-Protocol for Metadata Harvesting (OAI-PMH) defines a mechanism for harvesting records containing metadata from repositories. OAI-PMH offers a simple techni-cal option for data providers to make their metadata available to services, based on the open standards HTTP and XML. The metadata that is harvested may be in any format that is agreed by a community or by any discrete set of data and service providers, although the default format for exchanging metadata between institutional repositories and service providers is simple Dublin Core (DC). For many services based on harvesting repositories, this format has significant limitations. A well-known problem of simple Dublin Core is its lack of detail or granularity. For example, there are no separate elements for volume, issue and page.

3.4.1 Other descriptive Metadata Formats

Instead of Dublin Core (DC) other descriptive or bibliographic metadata formats can be used to obtain more granularity (Foulonneau & André, 2007).

Qualified Dublin Core [14]

This is not a metadata format but rather a list of DC terms that can be used in any application profile. No official schema exists for encoding qualified DC. In practice, a multiplicity of schemas has been created to use QDC. It is maintained by the Dublin Core Metadata Initiative.

MARC [15]

A set of metadata formats traditionally used in the library community to create and exchange bibliographic information. Multiple local implementations of MARC exist. MARCXML has been created from MARC21, merging USMARC and CAN/MARC. The MARCXML schema is maintained by the Library of Congress.

MODS [16]

Metadata Object Description Schema (MODS) is a schema for a bibliographic element set that may be used for a variety of purposes, and particularly for library applications. It includes a subset of MARC fields and uses language-based tags rather than numeric ones, in some cases regrouping elements from the MARC 21 bibliographic format. It is maintained at the Library of Congress.

Scholarly Works Application Profile (SWAP) [17]

SWAP (originally the EPrints Application Profile, renamed Scholarly Works Application Profile) is a Joint Information System Committee (JISC) initiative to create an application profile 'for describing scholarly publications (EPrints) held in institutional repositories'. Instead of defining new metadata elements for simple DC, it reengineers the design of metadata for EPrints.

---

[14] http://dublincore.org/documents/dcmi-terms/

[15] http://www.loc.gov/marc/

[16] http://www.loc.gov/standards/mods/

[17] http://www.ukoln.ac.uk/repositories/digirep/index/SWAP

The data model considers EPrints in the context of research activity. The model does not represent stable documents but a scholarly work that corresponds to one or more copies of that work and one or more agents that were involved in the creation of that work. In the SWAP model, the scholarly work is conceived as the result of a process in which a number of actors (creator of work, funding organisation, identifier) intervene.

3.4.2 XML containers
There are also a number of XML containers, instead of descriptive metadata formats, that include different type of metadata and (parts of) digital objects or links to digital objects.

METS

METS is a structured container of different types of metadata: descriptive, structural and administrative. It does not determine which metadata format(s) is/are going to be used for the description of the digital object. As a result, it is implemented with application profiles. However, a number of metadata formats have been endorsed as METS extensions, i.e. DC, MODS, PREMIS. It has been extensively used in the library community to represent and exchange information about complex objects, including a hierarchical representation of their structure, especially for digitised books. It is maintained by the Library of Congress.

DoMDL

The Document Model for Digital Library (DoMDL) is used in OpenDLib. OpenDLib is a Digital Library Service System that allows publishing or self-publishing, maintenance and dissemination of documents that conform to the DoMDL document model to represent multi-edition, structured, multimedia documents that can be disseminated in multiple manifestation formats.

MPEG21-DIDL

In the MPEG-21 Framework, complex digital objects are declared using the Digital Item Declaration Language (DIDL). DIDL is a subset of the MPEG-21 ISO standards. It includes the representation of the object as multiple metadata sets or pointers to multiple parts of the object. DIDL is more suitable as exchange format than METS for repositories, because each object or part of an object can have an identifier and a date stamp in DIDL. When a part of an object is renewed, the date stamp also changes and, due to a cascading effect, the date stamp of the whole DIDL document also does.

LOM, IMS CP and SCORM

LOM IEEE standard is developed for Learning Object Metadata (LOM). LOM is a metadata standard to describe educational resources. It is aimed at the exchange and reuse of learning objects. It contains many types of metadata for the inclusion of learning resources into Learning Management Systems. The IMS Global Learning Consortium has developed specifications for Learning Resource Metadata as well as for content packaging. IMS Content Packaging (IMS CP) is a standard for the assembly of resources, metadata and sequencing information into a learning object. The SCORM 1.2 profile extends IMS Content Packaging with sophisticated sequencing and Contents-to-LMS communication.

Data Documentation Initiative (DDI)

Enhanced Publications also need some other metadata formats or XML containers different from those mentioned above, e.g. to structure the associated data sets to publications. The Data Documentation Initiative (DDI) is an important format to structure data sets. The DDI is an XML specification for social science metadata that is being developed by an international group called the DDI Alliance. The bylaws of the Alliance mandate an open Public Review period for the latest draft release (version 3.0). DDI also has the potential to structure data sets from other scientific disciplines than the social sciences.

Metadata models or XML containers are also developed to structure data and data sets in specific scientific disciplines. For instance:

• MIDAS Heritage is the UK data standard for information about the historic environment (archaeology).
• NetCDF Climate and Forecast (CF) Metadata Convention defines metadata that provide a definitive description of what the data in each variable represents, and the spatial and temporal properties of the data.

3.5   Scholarly Communication

An Enhanced Publication may be seen as a type of compound object. It is not one file or a composition of several files, but consists of digital objects or resources that can be distributed over several locations. In DIDL the entities of an Enhanced Publication are digital items. In METS digital objects are modelled as tree structures, e.g. book with chapters with subchapters. Every node in the tree can be associated with descriptive/administrative metadata and individual/multiple files or portions thereof. For the description and structuring of an Enhanced Publication XML containers are essential.

Yet, the use of XML containers and metadata formats for data sets is just a starting point. In an earlier publication, Herbert van de Sompel proposed a more advanced notion of a scholarly communication system that would fully cover the way scholars work. Such a system would allow flexible composition of information units – text, data sets, images – and distributed services for the formation of new types of published results and new methods of collaborating. This results in a loosely coupled system based on an interoperability fabric where the units of scholarly communication may follow a variety of scholarly value chains.

A core component of this vision is a new notion of the scholarly document or publication. Rather than being static and text-based, this scholarly artefact combines data, text, images, and services flexibly in multiple ways regardless of their location and genre. This vision requires an interoperability fabric that is considerably richer than is provided by OAI-PMH. Rather than just allowing exchange of structured descriptive metadata, it needs to represent and exchange information about compound digital objects: their structure, lineage, and persistent identity. OAI-ORE is the model for such a vision.

Open Archives Initiative Object Reuse and Exchange (OAI-ORE)
OAI-ORE defines standards for the description and exchange of aggregations of Web resources. The World Wide Web is built upon the notion of atomic units of information ('resources') that are identified with URIs. In addition to these atomic units, aggregations of resources are often units of information in their own right.

The OAI-ORE specifications are based around the ORE Model. The ORE Model introduces the Resource Map enabling association of an identity with aggregations of resources and making assertions about their structure and semantics. The primary serialisation format for Resource Maps is a profile of Atom. Because the ORE Model is expressed in RDF, Resource Maps may also be serialised in any format capable of serializing RDF.

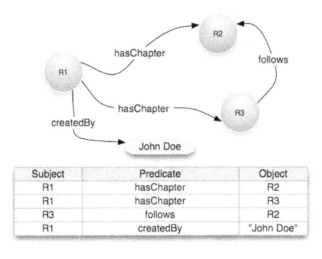

Subject	Predicate	Object
R1	hasChapter	R2
R1	hasChapter	R3
R3	follows	R2
R1	createdBy	"John Doe"

Figure 6a. Relationships between the resources

A Resource Map describes an Aggregation which is a set of resources, and possibly their types and relationships between the resources. Resources in the Aggregation are called Aggregated Resources. In order to be able to talk about the Aggregation on the Web, it must have a URI (say A-1). According version 0.2 of OAI-ORE this URI is constructed by appending #aggregation to the Resource Map URI, i.e. ReM-1#aggregation. This syntactic device ensures that there is a unique Aggregation resource for every Resource Map.

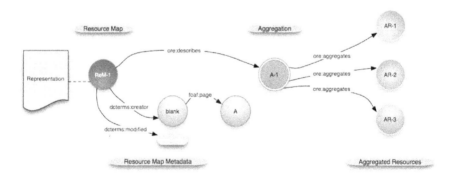

Figure 6b. Basic of the OAI-ORE model

Figure 6c shows a complete Resource Map with statements indicated as arrows from subject resource to object resource or literal.

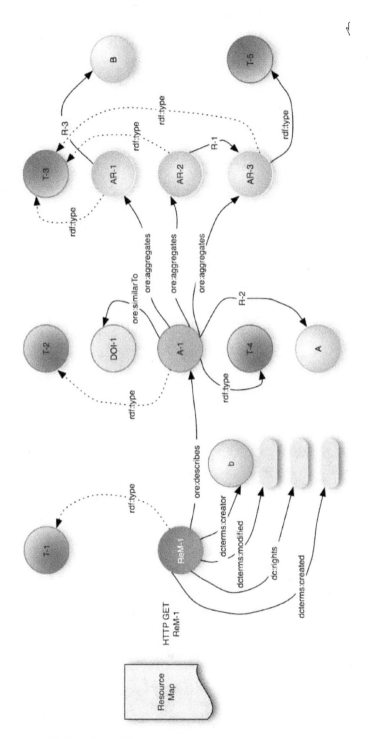

Figure 6. Model of OAI-ORE

43

4. Characteristic Features of Objects

Summary

A full registration requires a timestamp, a unique identifier, a resolver and in the case of a data set a universal numeric fingerprint. Scholarly objects should be provided with a unique citation to be traceable to the cited work.

All objects should clearly have a mark of peer review including quality and integrity standards. Concerning legal issues we can learn a lot from archives, which have dealt with data sets for many years, and have developed contracts for deposit and use.

To optimise the visibility of all objects of an Enhanced Publication, all objects should
- *be provided with a unique global identifier so they can be easily linked to and retrieved;*
- *be cited in such a way that citations can be easily found;*
- *be stored in a Unique Global Identifier;*
- *have a Universal Numeric Fingerprint and a Bridge service;*
- *be conceived in a resolver sustainable way, in which repositories are preferable to publishers' Web sites;*
- *be machine-readable, for indexing and using or reusing the materials;*
- *be freely available, for indexing and easy accessibility.*

Universities and research institutes should assume the responsibility of archiving the digital scholarly output of their organisation in a sustainable way. Repositories have a suitable harvesting infrastructure for archiving scholarly output in national libraries or archives; disciplinary repositories and the Dataverse Network should also be considered.

Repositories should enable provision of a complete reference to all deposited objects. Researchers who use the scholarly object can then properly cite the material. It is also very important to show the number of citations with the materials. This will reveal the importance of the research(er).

4.1   Introduction

Van de Sompel and Lagoze (2007) have suggested that the crucial functions of scholarly communication, being registration, certification, awareness, archiving and rewarding, should be re-implemented in a new context. A 'service hub' manages each function of the publication system. The service(s) needed determine which 'service hubs' are necessary and in which order (Herbert van de Sompel et al., 2004). In this section we look at each function of the publication system to see what is of importance for that particular function in composing an Enhanced Publication.

4.2   Registration

Registration is the most important function in the system of scholarly communication. It is necessary that discoveries, inventions and innovations are publicly registered and claimed. With proper registration, you can prove that a particular idea was yours, that you were the first. Altman and King (2007) propose that, besides the three traditional components author(s), date of publication and title, citations to numerical data should include three other components, a timestamp, a universal Numeric Fingerprint and a unique identifier. These components are necessary to identify a particular object unambiguously and to guarantee a stable location, easy retrieval and verification of the study.

4.2.1   Timestamp

The registration date is recorded by the journal publisher as the date the manuscript is received. It is important to look at the timing of registration and how this relates to the quality of what is to be registered (Herbert van de Sompel et al., 2004). Time-stamping is not only important for a publication but also for all other objects of scholarly communication, like data sets, images, movies, models, database queries (Sayeed Choudhury, 2008), and also for each original aggregation of objects.

4.2.2   Universal Numeric Fingerprint (UNF)

Normally it is easy to check whether two objects are the same or not, but with data sets this task may be quite complicated. Data correction, updating and maintenance follow separate curatorial mechanisms, if so at all. These mechanisms are not synchronised to those that manage the article literature (Lynch, 2007). Besides this we also need to guarantee and verify independently that the object has not changed in any meaningful way when the data storage format has changed. A Universal Numeric Fingerprint (UNF) solves these problems.

The UNF is a short, fixed-length string of numbers and characters that summarises all the content in the data set in a way that a change in any part of the data would produce a completely different UNF.

A UNF works by translating the data firstly into a canonical form with fixed degrees of numerical precision. Then it applies a cryptographic hash function to produce the short string. The advantage of canonicalisation is that UNFs, but not raw hash functions, are format-independent. They keep the same value even if the data set is moved between software programs, file storage systems, compression schemes, operating systems, or hardware platforms (Micah Altman & King, 2007).

A UNF differs from an ordinary file checksum in several important ways:
- UNFs are format independent. The UNF for the data will be the same regardless of whether the data is saved as R binary format, SAS formatted file, Stata formatted file, but file checksums will differ;
- UNFs are robust to insignificant rounding error. A UNF will also be the same if the data differs in non-significant digits; a file checksum will not;
- UNFs detect misinterpretation of the data by the statistical software. If the statistical software misreads the file, the resulting UNF will not match the original, but file checksums may match.

UNFs are strongly tamper resistant. Any accidental or intentional change to the data values will change the resulting UNF. Most file checksums and descriptive statistics detect only certain types of changes. UNF libraries are available for standalone use, for use in C++, and for use with other packages (Micah Altman, 2006). More information about the UNF can be found in the work of Altman et al. (2003) platforms (Micah Altman & King, 2007).

4.2.3 Unique (Global) Identifier (UGI)
Each unit of scholarly communication or aggregate thereof needs a unique identifier. This is important for all levels of scholarly communication: articles, modules, objects, queries and also for database objects (Seringhaus & Gerstein, 2007).

The Unique Global Identifier (UGI) is a short name or character string guaranteed to be unique that permanently identifies the data set, independently of its location. Altman and King (2007) allow any naming scheme as long as it identifies the object unambiguously, is globally unique, and is associated with a naming resolution service that takes the name as input and shows how to find one or more copies of the identical object.

They recommend the unique global identifier not to resolve to the object itself, but to a page containing the descriptive and structural metadata describing the object, presented in human-readable form to Web browsers. This metadata description page should include a link to the actual object, as well as a textual description of the object, the full citation in the format we will discuss below, complete documentation, and any other pertinent information. The advantage of this general approach is that identifiers in citations can always be resolved, even if the data are proprietary; require licensing agreements to be signed prior to access; are confidential; demand security clearance; are under temporary embargo until the authors execute their right of first publication, or for other reasons. With metadata description pages like these search engines can find data more easily. Metadata may follow emerging standards, or any other scheme (Micah Altman & King, 2007).

A list with identifiers and identifier resolution services from the e-bank Web site[18] is included in the Appendix of Part 1.

Resolver
Most Web browsers do not recognise global unique identifiers. According to Altman and King (2007) we need a 'bridge service'. This service is referred to as a Resolver of the identifier.

4.3   Certification

Certification establishes the validity of a registered scholarly claim. Mostly it takes the form of a peer-review process, conducted under the auspices of the journal publisher who certifies the claims made in the manuscript.

King (2007) thinks that not many journals with supplementary

---

[18] http://www.ukoln.ac.uk/projects/ebank-uk/data-citation/

48

materials have engaged in legal counsel to consider the potential liability surrounding the way they accept and distribute data. He discusses the fact that most journals merely post on their own websites whatever material authors submit, with no check by journal staff, no internal review board (IRB) approval, and not even any signed testimony by the author that distributing the data would not violate any laws, as an author is obliged to do on the copyright-transfer agreement for the publication. King remarks: "Publishers have well honed procedures for dealing with copyright and liability issues for printed matter, but these standard copyright assignment forms do not cover acquiring and distributing data off the printed page.". His advice is to learn from or work with the archives that have already dealt with these issues.

Some journals explicitly mention that supplementary materials are not peer reviewed and thus are a pure responsibility of the author. Lynch (2007) questions the relationships between traditional peer review and the material that underlies an article under review. He says that it is often unclear if the peer review of an article extends to peer review of the underlying data, even when journal policies are explicit on this. When linking objects we have to know something about quality and integrity standards. We need to be sure that within the law of proper scientific discourse, all knowledge presentations are equal (Joost G. Kircz, 2002).

Some claim that it is impossible to peer review materials other than publications. In some fields presently there is an effort to build peer-review systems around data, so data can be judged formally on qualities of coherence, design, consistency, reliability of access, and so on. In the UK, scientists and professional associations in the field of meteorology have joined forces to establish a new kind of electronic publication called a data journal, where practitioners can submit data sets for peer review and dissemination: the Overlay Journal Infrastructure for Meteorological Sciences (OJIMS). NCAS (Leeds) will provide feedback on how this will work from an editor's point of view and help write the reviewers guidelines (Arms & Larsen, 2007). Another example is the Journal of Visualised Experiments (JoVE)[19], a peer-reviewed journal for video-protocols.

---

[19] http://www.jove.com/

4.4   Awareness

Awareness allows actors in the scholarly system to be informed of new claims and findings. Authors want the maximum amount of visibility, authority and prestige to ensure the validity of their claim. This is unnecessarily restrained by the way publishers and repositories have organised the publishing environment. Supplementary materials are mostly handled as individual objects, even though they are sometimes closely related. As we will see, in most cases there is no link between related objects.

4.4.1   Current Practice

Supplementary materials are mostly contained within the publisher's domain. Publishers started enhancing publications with digital objects on the Web around 2000. An article from 2001 lists movies with the abstract[20]. In 2008 the same approach is used, for example at Elsevier and Blackwell[21]. This method of presenting supplementary materials, called publishing with the article, will help other researchers to gain easy access to them once the article itself is found. Some publishers (BioMedCentral and Nature) are now also using separate channels for supplementary materials. Nature has a special Web site Nature Multimedia[22] with streaming videos featuring discussion and analysis with scientists as they share their discoveries, pod casts with a free weekly audio show highlighting the best of the week in science, blog on which you can have your say on the news of the day, tools to find out how the novel use of programs like Google Earth can help scientists discover and share information and specials like interactive graphics, quizzes, video galleries, pictures and more.

BioMed Central publishes movies about some of their articles[23] on SciVee[24]. But SciVee presents more than movies. It features figures, supplementary materials, references, related pubcasts, tags, submitted by, rating, uploaded, views, comments, and add to favourites like digg

---

[20] H. Muller "Identification of states responsible for ATI enhancements in argon by their calculated wave functions" *Optics Express*, Vol. 8, Issue 2, pp. 44-50. http://www.opticsinfobase.org/abstract.cfm?URI=oe-8-2-44

[21] e.g. http://www.blackwell-synergy.com/doi/suppl/10.1111/j.1462-5822.2005.00576.x

[22] http://www.nature.com/nature/multimedia/

[23] e.g. http://www.biomedcentral.com/1471-2105/7/242

[24] e.g. http://www.scivee.tv/node/2727

IT, del.icio.us, Slashdot, Furl, Facebook, StumbleUpon, Newsvine, Technorati, Reddit, Magnolia, Blinklist, and Netscape. It also contains URL, comments, viewers' notes and copyrights concerning the movie. As well as with Scivee, the movie can also be found on YouTube[25].

Amazingly, BMC and Nature do not have an active link between articles[26] and movies[27] or podcasts[28]. On the SciVee Web site information about articles is not linked, and on the Nature Web site the reference only appears for a few seconds at the beginning of the movie; on the article 'homepage', in both cases no information whatsoever can be found about movies on the Scivee or Nature video Web sites. Applying our definition of an Enhanced Publication it can be said that these publishers own the building blocks, but do not use the opportunity to create an Enhanced Publication.

Very few journals were found that link to authors' institutional Web sites to show movies and tools, like the Journal of Interactive Media in Education[29]. It is surprising that after more than six years many links are still working, even though researchers and researcher groups within institutions come and go. Most objects could still be found, albeit sometimes via a roundabout route. Linking to authors' institutional Web sites should never be supported in our view, since every other solution, e.g. repositories, publisher's Web site and commercial databases, is much safer. Although a publisher like IOP (Wray, 2007) has declared that they would welcome to collaborate with repositories, especially for grey literature, we have found no connections to a repository on the publisher's Web site. Repositories on the other hand often refer to the official publication on the publisher's Web site.

We have seen that supplementary materials need not necessarily be linked to the publication. They can be found on several locations:
- Repository, institutional or disciplinary;
- Web site of the author's institution;
- Publisher's Web site;

---

[25] e.g. http://www.youtube.com/watch?v=V72stkORlgo

[26] article: http://dx.doi.org/10.1038/nature06669 (subscription needed).

[27] video: http://www.nature.com/nature/videoarchive/selfhealingrubber/ (free access).

[28] podcast: http://media.nature.com/download/nature/nature/podcast/v451/ n7181/nature-2008-02-21.mp3 (free access).

[29] http://www-jime.open.ac.uk/2002/8/

- Blogs and wikis, like Open Notebook Science[30];
- Database, like the Protein Data Bank.

The fact that the publication and supplementary materials are not linked reduces the visibility of the supplementary materials.

4.4.2 Model for the Future

We have seen that supplementary materials are hosted across several locations. They are managed in many different ways, and sometimes are not linked to the publication. What can be done to improve the visibility of the publication and the supplementary material?
- The publication and the related objects should both have a unique identifier to ensure they can be referenced;
- The links between the publication and the supplementary materials should be set up on both sides, from the publication to the supplementary materials and vice versa;
- The objects must be held at a trustworthy location and published on an open access basis, which will result in more downloads and more citations[31].

What locations are most suited to store supplementary materials? According to Lynch (2007) disciplinary repositories, national or international, are preferred. Journals are less suited:
- Not every journal accepts supplementary materials;
- Journals have no clear policy about preserving data or the tools to work with them;
- Some journals put constraints on the amount of data they will accept;
- Access to the data is for subscribers only;
- It is often unclear to what extent supplementary materials are part of the peer review.

The most important advantage of a disciplinary, as well as institutional, repository is the use of persistent identifiers that can be used to reference objects uniquely. None of the journals use persistent identifiers for supplementary materials. The benefits of international disciplinary repositories are that most of these communities have established norms, enforced by editorial policies. Journals can use

---

[30] The projects Useful chemistry/Open Notebook Science are using wikis and blogs to record research http://usefulchem.wikispaces.com/

[31] http://opcit.eprints.org/oacitation-biblio.html

repository identifiers to reference objects. However, the problem is that not all communities have a repository available. As yet, there are international repositories for only a few disciplines, like crystallography, astronomy, economics and molecular biology. Another problem is that these repositories do not accept all types of objects. In cases where objects cannot be stored in a disciplinary repository, an institutional repository may be a solution. The disadvantages of institutional repositories, set up as data providers, are that they lack easy centralised searching of material on a disciplinary basis, and that it may be very difficult to develop and maintain specialised discipline-specific software tools, as they are not intended as service providers (Lynch, 2007).

Other alternative locations for storing data sets are the Dataverse Network and data grid. In contrast to Lynch (who advises disciplinary repositories) King (2007) pleads for archiving data in the international Dataverse Network (DVN)[32]. This is a World Wide Virtual Network for data archiving, housed at the Institute for Quantitative Social Science (IQSS) at the Harvard-MIT Data Center. Coding of the DVN software began in 2006, but it is a continuation of the earlier Virtual Data Center (VDC) project (1999-2006) which was collaboration between the Harvard-MIT Data Center and Harvard University Library. The current DVN offers many features, uses many standards and is not intended for social science data only. A data grid is a grid-computing system that controls sharing and management of large volumes of distributed data. These systems are often, but not always, combined with computational grid-computing systems. Many scientific and engineering applications require access to large volumes of distributed data, terabytes or petabytes. Current large-scale data grid projects include the Biomedical Informatics Research Network (BIRN), the Southern California Earthquake Center (SCEC), and the Real-time Observatories, Applications, and Data management Network (ROADNet), all of which use of the SDSC Storage Resource Broker as the underlying data grid technology. These applications require widely distributed access to data by many people in many places. The data grid creates virtual collaborative environments that support distributed but coordinated scientific and engineering research[33].

Another question is whether data should be stored at multiple locations.

---

[32] http://thedata.org/
[33] source: http://en.wikipedia.org/wiki/Data_grid

LOCKSS[34] (Lots of Copies Keep Stuff Safe) is open-source software that provides librarians with an easy and inexpensive way to collect, store, preserve, and provide access to their own, local copy of authorised content. According to Lynch (2007) repeated publication of the same data is clearly undesirable. The right approach would be citation or similar forms of reference. Therefore, it should be very easy to link to data, including data in databases like the Human Genome Project[35]. Using the Van de Sompel and Lagoze model (2007), duplication of objects will not be necessary. The unique persistent link is sufficient to reuse the object. It even offers the possibility of 'virtual publication' in which combining objects can express a new idea without duplicating the objects[36]. This may be considered as a 'virtual publication' as all parts are found at different locations.

Use or reuse of publications or parts of them improves visibility and is also part of the reward for publication. For this, one should know what access rights are applicable to an object, article, aggregates. Who is the owner, and what rights apply. Creative Commons, copyright, transferred copyright? Although free and open access to all materials is normally preferable because of more visibility, it is neither always feasible nor necessary for the purpose of guaranteeing public distribution of quantitative information. Those who wish to access the objects can reasonably be asked to fulfil whatever authorisation requirements the original author needed to meet in order to acquire, distribute, and archive it in the first place. This may include signing a licensing agreement such as agreeing to respect confidentiality pledges made to research participants, signing the equivalent of a guest book or belonging to an institution with a membership to the archive. Different requirements may apply to different objects (King, 2007).

Rights for articles are clearly stated on all publishers' Web sites. For most supplementary materials this is not the case. For most materials no copyright owner is stated. Most toll-access publishers give no access to the supplementary materials, which is surprising because the

---

[34] http://www.lockss.org

[35] http://www.ornl.gov/hgmis/home.html

[36] As has been done in the NSDL Science Literacy Maps: Concept maps for science and math. education (http://NDSL.org). The service is helping teachers to connect concepts, standards, and NSDL resources but also uses (parts of) objects from other repositories, for example:
http://strandmaps.nsdl.org/?id=SMS-MAP-1594

materials are not part of the peer-review process. Blackwell states: "supplementary material will be published as submitted and will not be corrected or checked for scientific content, typographical errors or functionality. Although hosted on Blackwell Synergy, the responsibility for scientific accuracy and file functionality remains entirely with the authors. A disclaimer will be displayed to this effect with any supplementary material published.". Contrary to this statement the disclaimer cannot always be found on the Web site or on the supplementary materials. Only a few publishers (e.g. Nature) give access to the supplementary materials as well.

In addition to the access barriers, which will make it difficult to link between the worldwide results of scientific research, formats create another problem. In most cases it would be much more interesting having also the data on which a graph was based. Another problem is that not all PDF files can be searched as they are sometimes saved as images. These image files will never be machine-readable even when we have the right to access the file. To make data mining possible, repositories should require data being as 'raw' as possible.

4.5   Archiving

Archiving aims to preserve scholarly materials over time. In the past, libraries took care of publishers' paper materials. Should libraries also take care of publishers' digital supplementary materials? We believe that universities and research institutions should take responsibility for archiving their own digital scholarly materials in which they have invested. This holds in particular for supplementary materials, as publishers are not clear about archiving these. Only a few publishers guarantee that they will continue to support the accepted submission types of supplementary materials, now and in the future.

We know that researchers centuries from now need to be able to find supplementary material, access it, ascertain that it is the supplementary material associated with the article in question, and verify that it contains the same information that the author originally provided. Of course updates and new versions are desirable for some purposes, but the original version associated with the article must always remain available. The Version Identification Framework[37] (VIF)

---

[37] http://www.lse.ac.uk/library/vif/index.html

provides practical advice and recommendations to authors and content creators, repository managers and those involved with repository software on how to identify versions better.

We will need to follow procedures that ensure that the results of research will remain valid in the indefinite future, regardless of changes in methods of data distribution and network access, data storage formats, statistical and database software, operating systems, and computer hardware (King, 2007).

As a result of issues identified in UKOLN's 'Dealing with Data[38] report, the Digital Curation Centre in the UK has recently set up a Research Data Management Forum[39] to support the exchange of experience and expertise in the management and preservation of research data output.

Are libraries prepared to do the job? To keep the information accessible by migration or emulation libraries should cooperate on a national, European or international level. In the Netherlands for instance, libraries and research institutions can archive publications at the National Library of the Netherlands and data sets or images at Data Archiving and Networked Services (DANS) or the 3TU Data Centre of the Technical Universities in the Netherlands. The Dataverse Network (DVN) should also be considered. Libraries should help their organisations to develop policies on archiving.

4.6   Rewarding

Researchers reward each other by citation or when their material is published in a high impact journal. As is already pointed out, it is obvious that visibility enhances the impact of a publication, since a more visible publication generally will be downloaded and cited more often.

Metrics have been developed on the basis of citations to measure the performance of the research or the researcher. These metrics only count publications. That is why Seeber (2008) criticises citations in supplementary materials, which cannot be found in Web of Science. He

---

[38]http://www.jisc.ac.uk/whatwedo/programmes/programme_digital_repositories/ project_dealing_with_data.aspx

[39] http://www.dcc.ac.uk/data-forum/

56

suggests adding the references to the article instead of to the supplementary materials. However, publications and data sets should be seen as two separate objects of scholarly communication with their own references. The solution should be to make the references in the supplementary materials visible.

Separating publications and supplementary materials is important, as citation credit should be given to the right objects. That object can be the original publication but also another unit of scholarly communication. Researchers should be rewarded for the measurements, images, tools, peer review, comments and database annotations they have published (Fink & Bourne, 2007; Seringhaus & Gerstein, 2007). Using clear and unique citations to all objects would give credit to them. This applies also to scholarly output.

The data citation model of King (2007) offers proper recognition to authors as well as permanent identification through the use of global, persistent identifiers instead of URLs, which may change frequently. The Dataverse Network provides a unique reference to the data after depositing. After uploading, the author is issued a formal citation to the data, including a unique global identifier, a universal numeric fingerprint, and the other components, to be used in the author's article and to be cited in other publications (King, 2007). When data can be stored with this proper recognition to authors as well as permanent identification it will be possible to publish raw data and leave the analyses to other researchers. In this way credit can be given for the data that has been measured and/or analyzed.

Marcondes (2005) raises the question of why we do not use qualified citation. This is a citation in which the reasons to cite and the relationship between this specific scientific article and its citations are made explicit.

5. Relations

Summary

Instead of inserting an URL, as almost all publishers do nowadays, it is also possible to provide links with a 'meaning' in which the logical connection of terms establishes interoperability between parts of an Enhanced Publication. However, for the parts of an Enhanced Publication to interact in a semantic way, we need servers that expose existing data systems using the RDF standards, documents 'marked up' and ontologies, and authors must be asked for extra effort.

Three models can help to shape an environment for Enhanced Publications.

- *The DCMI Abstract Model can give a better understanding of the kinds of descriptions that are encoded, and how to facilitate better mappings and cross-syntax translations;*
- *The CIDOC CRM has shown how a successful ontology has been set up; that it can be used to support integration, not only in cultural heritage but also in a large range of different domains including e-science and biodiversity; that it can help to reduce development time; that it improves system quality, and provides basic semantic interoperability for free;*
- *ORE Vocabulary and Fedora Relationship ontology have defined a default set of common relationships that can be refined or extended.*

The conclusion is that ontologies should be used in the environment of Enhanced Publications and that OWL helps to make ontologies compatible.

5.1   Introduction

In the text of a publication or an Enhanced Publication authors can refer to research data and extra materials. Referring may be done manually but also through automated or semi automated semantic linking. Enhanced Publications may also import data or metadata from other systems, in order to complement a publication.

59

5.2   State of the Art

If authors wish to refer in the text to an annex containing research data and/or extra materials, they are required by the publisher to use a standard format for this reference, for example the phrase "see Electronic Annex 1 in the online version of this article.". The production department of the publisher will insert the relevant URL at the typesetting stage, by means of a hyperlink after this statement. Publishers currently only provide a one-way link from the article to the supplementary material, but never vice versa.

We have found that only one publisher (the American Astronomical Society, AAS) provides an extensive system of links between the literature and other external online information. The basis for this system is the identification of data sets. All astronomical data centres assign unique identifiers to each set of data. It is up to the data centre to decide what they consider a data set: one spectrum, one exposure or a set of exposures of the same object at different wavelengths. In some cases, data sets are defined by the query parameters to a database query. Some data centres also provide the means for authors to define a collection of data sets that they used in an article and to give this collection a unique identifier. The main requirement for data set identifiers is that they have to be unique and permanent. This means that the data centres have to agree to recognise published identifiers in perpetuity (Eichhorn et al., 2007).

Publishers mostly include the links manually. One exception is the addition of hyperlinks in lists of literature references. For instance, Crossref[40] automatically provides the DOIs for research content in the publication. The Crossref database covers millions of articles and other content items from several hundred scholarly and professional publishers.

If we want to create Enhanced Publications in the repository environment using OAI-ORE, we can build on a part of the current infrastructure and some of the current standards. All objects with a URI, for example a publication and a data set, can already be connected; and some parts of the current infrastructure and standards can be converted to the new infrastructure and standards: DIDL containers can be converted to Resource Maps to which we can add

---

[40] http://www.crossref.org/

URIs. Another example is the Digital Author Identifier, which is used in the Netherlands. Aggregates can be made on DAI[41]. An author's new publications will be automatically added to the publication list (Place, 2008).

5.3   Semantic Publishing

As we have seen, Enhanced Publications consist of heterogeneous data, heterogeneous information types, information from different disciplines, different languages. The Semantic Web provides a common framework that allows data to be shared and reused across application, enterprise, and community boundaries.

Professionals and researchers in the field require that the descriptive information is sufficiently detailed and precise. For this purpose, interoperability of the parts of an Enhanced Publication is required not only at the syntactic and system level but also at the more semantic level. Semantic integration is the process of using a conceptual representation of data and of their relationships to eliminate possible ambiguities. The problem is that the same elements may express different meanings for different cases and types. Ontologies offer the solutions to the semantic heterogeneity problems and can be used in integration architectures as a global schema to which metadata from different sources can be mapped (Kakali et al., 2007).

Machine-readable descriptions should enable content managers to add meaning to the content, i.e. to describe the structure of the knowledge we have about that content. The semantic web makes it possible, instead of only inserting plain URLs in the text, to set up a logical connection of terms that establishes interoperability between the different parts of an Enhanced Publication.

The semantic web has several components.

- *Uniform Resource Identifiers (URI).* Identifier, used to identify resources on Internet and so they are central to the Semantic Web. Computer scientists may classify a URI as a locator (URL), or a name (URN), or both.

---

[41] http://<author_service>/rem/atom/<dai>

- *Extensible Markup Language (XML).* Syntax, provides an elemental syntax for content structure within documents, yet associates no semantics with the meaning of the content contained within.

- *XML Schema.* Language, for providing and restricting the structure and content of elements contained within XML documents.

- *Resource Description Framework (RDF).* Data interchange format, a formal description of concepts, terms, and relationships within a given knowledge domain. It is a representation language for Universal Resource Identifiers (URIs). The semantic web is based on the Resource Description Framework (RDF).

- *RDF Schema (RDFS).* Taxonomy, a structured vocabulary for describing properties and classes of RDF-based resources, with semantics for generalised-hierarchies of such properties and classes.

- *Web Ontology Language (OWL).* Ontology, adds more vocabulary for describing properties and classes, and describes the function and relationship of each of the components above. Ontologies can refer by virtue or URIs.

URIs have a global scope and are interpreted consistently across contexts. Associating a URI with a resource means that anyone can link to it, refer to it or retrieve a representation of it. They provide the grounding for both objects and relations. All scientific objects should be mapped for reuse into the system of URIs. Anything that can be identified with a Uniform Resource Identifier (URI) can be described. So the semantic web can reason about animals, people, places, and ideas.

HTML describes documents and the links between them. RDF, OWL, and XML, by contrast, can describe arbitrary things such as people, meetings, or airplane parts. Tim Berners-Lee calls the resulting network of Linked Data the Giant Global Graph, in contrast to the HTML-based World Wide Web ("Semantic Web", 2009).

5.4   Tools

Tools for publishing papers on the web can automatically help users to include more machine-readable markup in the papers they produce. With current XML-tools[42] it is already possible to assert that some part of a document is about an experiment. A new set of languages and tools[43] is now being developed to create machine-readable content to make the publications widely available. According to Berners-Lee & Hendler (2001) authors will need to be asked to make some extra effort, in repayment for major new functionality:

- Experimental results on the web can be shared with (trusted) colleagues, outside the context of a research paper;
- More detailed information on the research subjects (chemicals, reactions, location, species);
- The semantic web can break down the walls between disciplines, since it can bring together those concepts that different disciplines have in common.

To enhance the usability and usefulness of the Web and its interconnected resources we need servers which expose existing data systems using the RDF standards, documents 'marked up' and ontologies.

5.4.1   Markup Language
Markup Language is one of the languages that give more detailed information on the research subject and the structure of the object, being embedded formal metadata in documents. Examples are the 'deep structure' (XML) of an article and links with a defined relation to other online objects cited in the article. Marcondes recommends use of qualified citations, in which the reasons to cite and the relationship between this specific scientific article and its citations are made explicit (<reason_to_cite>). He claims that the use of these XML-tags can enhance the scientific communication process, permitting semantic retrieval, critical enquiry, semantic citation, comparison, coherence verification and validation of a scientific article (Marcondes, 2005).

---

[42] http://www.nature.com/nature/webmatters/xml/xml.html

[43] List of Semantic Publishing Tools:

http://esw.w3.org/topic/HCLS/ScientificPublishingTaskForce;

http://esw.w3.org/topic/TaskForces/CommunityProjects/LinkingOpenData/PublishingTools

5.4.2 Ontology

An ontology is a formal representation of a set of concepts within a domain and the relationships between those concepts. It provides a shared vocabulary, which can be used to model a domain. A domain is to be understood as the type of objects and/or concepts that exist, and their properties and relations. Ontologies are attempts to define parts of the data world more carefully, and to allow mapping and interactions between data held in different formats as can be the case in Enhanced Publications. Ontologies are always developed, managed, and endorsed by practice communities, and defined through a careful, explicit process that attempts to remove ambiguity (Shadbolt, Berners-Lee, & Hall, 2006).

Although ontologies are usually developed for specific information domains, and are used to formally represent data in such domains, they share many structural similarities, regardless of the language in which they are expressed. Most ontologies describe individuals or instances, classes or concepts, attributes, and relations.

The Web Ontology Language[44] (OWL) is a semantic markup language specially developed for publishing and sharing ontologies on the World Wide Web. OWL is intended to provide a language that can be used to describe the concepts definitions and the relations between them that are inherent in digital documents and applications. Ontologies can become distributed, as OWL allows ontologies to refer to terms in other ontologies. OWL is developed as a vocabulary extension of RDF. By providing additional vocabulary along with formal semantics, OWL facilitates greater machine interpretability of Web content than that supported by XML, RDF, and RDF Schema (RDF-S) (McGuinness & van Harmelen, 2004).

Since we are interested in models that can be of use for Enhanced Publications, we will look in more detail at four models. We will consider the DCMI Abstract Model, the CIDOC Conceptual Reference Model (CRM), ORE Vocabulary, and Fedora Relationship Ontology.

DCMI Abstract Model

The DCMI Abstract Model specifies the components and constructs used in Dublin Core metadata. It describes an information structure called a DC 'description set' and specifies how those description sets are to be

---

[44] http://www.w3.org/TR/owl-features/

interpreted. The DCMI Abstract Model is based on the Resource Description Framework (RDF) and builds on work by the World Wide Web Consortium (W3C). The model consists of a resource model, a description set model, a vocabulary model, descriptions, description sets, records, values, semantics and guidelines. It is an information model that is independent of any particular encoding syntax. This model has shown that it can help understanding of the kinds of descriptions that are encoded, and that it can facilitate the development of better mappings and cross-syntax translations (Powell, Nilsson, Naeve, Johnston, & Baker, 2007).

CIDOC conceptual Reference Model

The aim of the CIDOC Conceptual Reference Model (CRM)[45] is to provide a reference model and information standard for museums and other cultural heritage institutions to describe their collections and related business entities, to improve information sharing. For that the CIDOC CRM provides definitions and a formal structure for describing the implicit and explicit concepts and relationships used in cultural heritage documentation "to facilitate the integration, mediation and interchange of heterogeneous cultural heritage information, allowing data to be combined from heterogeneous data sources in a meaningful way and without loss of detail". The model is not prescriptive, but provides a controlled language to describe common high-level semantics that allow for information integration at the schema level. The names of classes and properties of a CRM-compatible form may be translated into any local language, but the identifying codes must be preserved. By virtue of this classification, data can be understood as propositions of a kind declared by the CRM about real world facts, such as "Object x forms part of: Object y". By adopting formal semantics the pre-conditions for machine-to-machine interoperability and integration have been established.

It looks like CIDOC CRM will become an important information standard and reference model for Semantic Web initiatives, and will serve as a guide for data modelling more generally ("CIDOC Conceptual Reference Model," 2007). CIDOC CRM can be used by software applications that use RDF, XML, DAML+OIL, OWL and others[46]. Formal mappings have been established for some data structures, including Dublin Core.

---

[45] http://cidoc.mediahost.org

[46] CIDOC CRM Tools and RDF mappings http://cidoc.ics.forth.gr/tools.html

Doerr et al. (2007) claim that the CIDOC CRM is well suited as a new standard for knowledge sharing. They have investigated to what extent and in which form global schema integration is feasible, and they have demonstrated the ability of the CRM to support integration in a large range of different domains including cultural heritage, e-science and biodiversity. Conceptual modelling on the basis of such well-tested core ontology reduces development time drastically. It improves system quality, and it also provides basic semantic interoperability, more or less for free. They have written a tutorial that addresses part of the technology needed for information aggregation and integration in the global information environment. The tutorial first addresses require-ments and semantic problems to integrate digital information into large scale, meaningful networks of knowledge that support not only access to source documents but also use and reuse of integrated information. The core ontologies of relationships in particular are fundamental to schema integration. They play a completely different role compared to the specialist terminologies that are used within a discipline.

ORE Vocabulary

The Open Archives Initiative (OAI) develops and promotes interopera-bility standards that aim to facilitate the efficient dissemination of content. OAI has its roots in the open access and institutional repository movements. Open Archives Initiative Object Reuse and Exchange (OAI-ORE) has defined standards for the description and exchange of aggre-gations of Web resources. They have described a glossary of terms and the vocabularies needed to describe items of interest and express the relationships between them within the OAI-ORE context. A guiding prin-ciple is to reuse existing vocabularies when possible for terms that are not specific and fundamental to the ORE model, for example Dublin Core Metadata Initiative (DCMI) and the Resource Description Framework (RDF). For vocabularies not described by OAI-ORE or other existing vocabularies, domain specific vocabularies should be created and maintained by their respective communities (Lagoze et al., 2008).

The ORE Vocabulary Definition defines and describes the ORE specific terms. These terms are within the ORE namespace and are used to construct ORE Resource Maps.

ORE Vocabulary, ORE Classes

A semantic class should be assigned to resources that are described using ORE. This helps applications to understand what the aggregation contains and represents. For example, an aggregation of journal articles could be typed as a journal, a journal issue, a journal volume, an overlay journal, a special issue of a journal, a reading list, a citations list, and so on. The core objects or entities of interest within the OAI-ORE context are Aggregation, AggregatedResource, Proxy and ResourceMap.

ORE Vocabulary, ORE Relationships

Relationships may refer to another object, but the object of the relation may also be a literal value rather than another resource. Some abstract concepts are both, for example the rights statement could be inline as a string or a reference to an external resource. The discussion is shaped by vocabulary, rather than any distinction as to the subject or object of the relationship. Relationships that exist between entities or from an entity to a literal value: aggregates; isAggregatedBy; describes; isDescribedBy; lineage; proxyFor; proxyIn; and similarTo (Lagoze et al., 2008).

Fedora Relationship

The Fedora repository system has defined a default set of common relationships in the Fedora relationship ontology[47] (actually, a simple RDF schema), which defines a set of common generic relationships useful in creating digital object networks:

```
<isPartOf> <hasPart>
<isConstituentOf> <hasConstituent>
<isMemberOf> <hasMember>
<isSubsetOf> <hasSubset>
<hasCollectionMember>
<isDerivationOf> <hasDerivation>
<isDependentOf> <hasDependent>
<isDescriptionOf> <hasDescription>
<isMetadataFor> <hasMetadata>
<isAnnotationOf> <has Annotation>
<hasEquivalent>
```

These relationships can be refined or extended. Also, communities can define their own ontologies to encode relationships among Fedora digital objects ("Fedora Digital Object Relationships - Fedora Repository Release 3.0," 2008).

---

[47] http://www.fedora.info/definitions/1/0/fedora-relsext-ontology.rdfs

6. Current Repository Projects

Summary

If we look at the current products of traditional publishers like Elsevier and Springer, no integrated metadata models, XML containers or models for scholarly communications are used. Enhanced Publications are mostly just articles with additional files that contain data sets and multimedia material.

In the eCrystals Federation Project metadata about the crystal, like chemical formula of the crystallised material, molecule name, and authors, are stored in simple Dublin Core (DC). Additional chemical information is stored as Qualified Dublin Core. The derived data sets are stored as files in the repository together with the files for representations or images of the crystal and the molecule. The eCrystals Federation Project is based on the eBank project which exports metadata using the OAI-PMH protocol in two different metadata formats, simple DC and METS. The eCrystals Federation Project will be a test bed for the OAI-ORE model (Atom Publishing Model), as DC and METS are too limited.

The ARROW/DART/ARCHER strategy does not require the use of a single metadata schema to describe all digital objects stored in the repository. Multiple formats to suit individual content models can be supported. OCLC and ARROW are working together to test a mapping tool developed by OCLC called the Interoperability Core that is based on mappings and crosswalks between different metadata formats. Metadata can be stored and searched in the native format generated by the community of practice. Using this strategy ARROW can be populated with metadata from a variety of formats and through various mappings converted to an interoperable core that can then be converted to DC for harvesting via OAI-PMH by resource discovery services.

If we look at all the above described projects, repositories are used not only to store and ensure permanent access to publications of multiple types, such as articles, conference-papers, reports and books, but also to store and offer access to data sets, research data, images and multimedia. Metadata varies from DC to METS or individual content models for community specific applications. Links between objects in repositories are now mostly bidirectional. Repositories may be discipline-specific or more generally oriented like institutional repositories.

In future, repositories will more and more be used for all kind of data: different publication types, data sets, research data and extra materials, e.g. images, video. Enhanced Publications can be created on the basis of the objects held in repositories. The internal format and repository infrastructure must be flexible enough to deliver common metadata formats such as DC, MODS, DIDL or METS, or more community specific metadata formats. Above all repository infrastructures must support the OAI-ORE model. The development of systems to manage the complete cycle of e-research and scientific collaboration will be based on repository infrastructures.

6.1   The eCrystals Federation

The eCrystals Federation Project[48] aims to establish a worldwide and sustainable federation of open data repositories supporting Open Science in crystallography. This new project is a continuation of the eBank UK project[49]. The earlier project developed the eCrystals archive[50], an OAI-PMH compliant repository populated with a number of crystallography data sets. The repository is based on modified EPrints 3 software. It also developed a demonstrator for an aggregation service, using ARC for harvesting and Cheshire for indexing and searching, showing the potential for searching across data set and publication metadata. Phase 3 included a scoping study for an international eCrystals federation.

The sub-discipline of crystallography was originally chosen by eBank because it has a well-defined data creation workflow and a tradition of sharing results data in an internationally accepted standard, the Crystallographic Information File (CIF) adopted by the International Union of Crystallography (IUCr). The projects are funded by JISC[51] and can be seen as demonstrators for applications in other areas.

---

[48] http://wiki.ecrystals.chem.soton.ac.uk/index.php/Main_Page

[49] http://www.ukoln.ac.uk/projects/ebank-uk/

[50] http://ecrystals.chem.soton.ac.uk/

[51] http://www.jisc.ac.uk/

The eCrystals archive stores data from crystallographic analyses as metadata records and files. When a crystal is analysed, terabytes of data are generated and held in proprietary formats. From this, data sets and data presentations can be derived which are substantially smaller and more interoperable. These derived data sets are stored as files in the repository together with the files for representations or images of the crystal and the molecule. The metadata for the crystal, e.g. chemical formula for the crystallised material, molecule name, and authors, is stored as simple Dublin Core. Additional chemical information like International Chemical Identifier, is stored as Qualified Dublin Core. In the eBank project, links were made from the metadata record to scientific articles and vice versa.

As part of the eBank UK project an Application Profile[52] was developed, configured according to the Dublin Core Metadata Initiative Abstract Model and the Dublin Core Application Profile Guidelines. The eCrystals project aims to harmonise the application profiles from participating repositories operating on different platforms like EPrints, DSpace, Fedora & ReciprocalNet, and establish a core Federation Application Profile and mappings. In the first phase of the project, only institutions using the EPrints platform will be included; the second phase roll out will include other platforms. Aggregation services will be examined and implemented at a national and international level.

The eCrystals Federation project aims to make a substantial contribution to a repository-based e-infrastructure for research data. Its broad outline will be as follows:

Metadata and data sets will be entered into institutional data repositories. Aggregators will harvest the metadata and provide services, and links will be made to scientific publications. So articles by the scientists depositing data could be held either in institutional or subject repositories. Bidirectional linking to publishers' 'repositories' with scientific articles will be examined and implemented. Within eBank DOIs were used to link data; other options may be considered for the eCrystals Federation project.

The project also aims to enable the Federation to interoperate with international subject archives IUCr and CCDC (Cambridge Crystallographic Data Centre) and other third party harvesters.

---

[52] http://www.ukoln.ac.uk/projects/ebank-uk/schemas/profile/

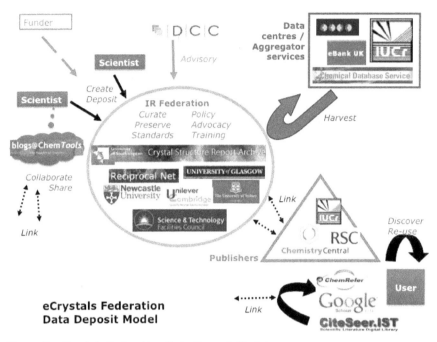

Figure 7. eCrystals Federation Data Deposit Model

The eCrystals Federation will be a test bed for the OAI-ORE model (Atom Publishing Model), as DC and METS are too limited. This is likely to be a key role for the project.

6.2 ARROW, DART and Archer at Monash University

Monash University is a large university with 55,000 students in various countries, among which are Australia (its main location), Malaysia, and South-Africa. University policy and the institutional context of an e-research infrastructure for institutional repositories are impressive.

Two years ago a start was made with the development of an Information Management Strategy in close cooperation with researchers and with the full support of higher management and the whole university. This led to the establishment of an E-research Centre to support researchers with e-research. Data size can vary greatly, but in some cases it is extremely large, e.g. Synchrotron 1 terabyte per day, Astronomy 12 terabyte per day.

Three national projects play an important part. The ARROW project aims at developing the management of scientific output in repositories. The DART project focuses on the development of solutions for a complete cycle of e-research: doing experiments, data analysis, publishing, learning. As a result data sets, storing data sets, preprints, and reports are generated. ARCHER is a continuation of DART aiming to become a production service for the national e-research environment (Treloar & Groenewegen, 2007).

As an example, the whole cycle of the analysis of and publication about a protein structure can be captured. The data sets generated by the analysis are eventually stored in the repository and linked to the scientific article on this protein structure.

It is thought necessary to store data for the following reasons:
- Data is holy;
- Data validation and validation of the scientific article;
- Some data elements could not be analyzed. Perhaps others are able to do this;
- Examples of data sets for those who develop analysis methods.

The institutional and centralised approach resulted in a central data storage facility, called Large Research Data Storage (LaRDS). Researchers are given 100 gigabyte, and if they want more than this, a one-off fee is payable.

For individual research, shared research and public domain, different storage systems are created. For the institutional repository in the public domain FEDORA is used with VITAL from VTLS. The major challenge in an IR is how to deal with large files, since for a protein analysis a sub file may already contain 36 gigabyte (Treloar, Groenewegen, & Harboe-Ree, 2007).

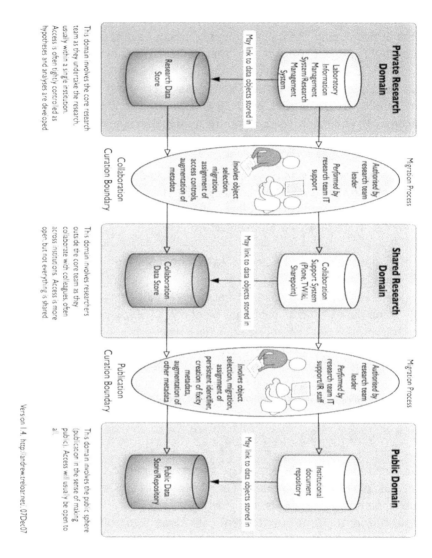

Figure 8. Different storage systems for individual research, shared research and public domain

6.3 eSciDoc Project

eSciDoc[53] is a shared project of the Max Planck Society and FIZ Karlsruhe, funded by the Federal Ministry of Education and Research

---

[53] http://www.escidoc-project.de

74

(BMBF) in Germany, with the aim of developing a platform for communication and publication in scientific research organisations. The eSciDoc project is intended to:

- Ensure permanent access to the research results and research materials of the Max-Planck Society and seamless integration within eSciDoc as well as integration into an emerging, global, electronic knowledge space;
- Provide effective opportunities for access to information for scientists of the Max-Planck Society and their work groups;
- Support scientific collaboration in future eScience scenarios.

eSciDoc Solutions

The first eSciDoc solution, publication management, will provide basic functionalities and user interfaces for the submission of publication data of multiple types like article, conference-paper, poster, report, and book, along with the metadata needed for efficient retrieval and long-term archiving. The second solution developed in the eSciDoc project, the scholarly workbench, is aimed at providing a generic solution for communities in the arts and humanities, to store their digital artefacts and make them 'processable' and reusable within a collaborative environment.

Infrastructure

The eSciDoc infrastructure is composed of middleware that encapsulates the repository and implements services in all layers of the service-oriented architecture relevant to the eSciDoc system. The core infrastructure is mainly built from existing open-source software packages. The eSciDoc content repository is based on Fedora. Fedora comes with a semantic store, which enables efficient administration of statements about objects and their relations, expressed in RDF (Resource Description Framework). Related objects form a graph, which can then be queried or used to infer new facts, based on existing RDF.

Metadata

The eSciDoc system supports various metadata schema or profiles. In fact, the basic services take a metadata-agnostic approach. They accept every well-formed XML tree as metadata record.

6.4   Imag(in)ing the Shuilu Temple in China

In this two-year project a very special and rare Shuilu temple in China was digitised. Recordings were made in 2D (TIFF) and 3D (Flash VR). Data totals circa 1.5 TERABYTE. Digital recordings were annotated by scientists. The aim is to enter this data in FEDORA and make them available using Fedora's image content model. However, this is not sufficient. For Fedora it is first necessary to:

- Adapt and develop various content models;
- Adapt and develop rich object to object relations;
- Develop standard and specific access mechanisms, in Fedora terms called disseminators, to show the right dynamic views, possibly using tools like Panorama viewer;
- Provide support to link to literature and annotations.

The aim is, among other things, to develop a number of standard content models and disseminators for Fedora.

6.5   SPECTRa: Chemistry Teaching and Research Data

The principal aim of the project Submission, Preservation and Exposure of Chemistry Teaching and Research Data (SPECTRa) was to facilitate the high-volume ingest and subsequent reuse of experimental data via institutional repositories, using the DSpace platform, by developing Open Source software tools which could easily be incorporated within chemists' workflows. It focused on three distinct areas of chemistry research: synthetic organic chemistry, crystallography and computational chemistry. One of SPECTRa's technology requirements was to find a suitable way of packaging data, i.e. to associate a number of data files together with some technical and descriptive metadata. The main alternatives were to use RDF, METS or MPEG21-DIDL. Of the three, METS was chosen because:

- It was the simplest technology that met the requirements;
- It had already been adopted by the eBank project;
- DSpace supports a METS profile as its primary package format.

6.6   StORe project: Source-to-Output Repositories

The StORe project seeks to address the area of interactions between output repositories of research publications and source repositories of primary research data. The functionality required by researchers in both types of repository is determined via user surveys identifying options for increasing the value of using primary data in source repositories as well as at the point where researchers submit papers to output repositories or download papers from them. This two-year project is multidisciplinary in scope, embracing seven scientific domains: archaeology, astronomy, biochemistry, biosciences, chemistry, physics and social sciences. Dublin Core is used as the metadata format and linking is achieved via bidirectional URLs between the publications and data sets.

7. Conclusion

An Enhanced Publication is a publication that is enhanced with research data as evidence of the research, extra materials to illustrate or to clarify or post-publication data like commentaries and ranking. Some publishers offer one or two of these categories with their official publications. Elsevier and Blackwell publications can have research data with the official publication, and Nature publications can have research data and also extra material, such as movies. It is surprising that Nature and BMC publish extra materials like movies separately from the publication, without even a link between these related objects. The reader of the article misses out on the movie, and the viewer of the movie remains unaware of the article. Only one publisher, PLoS, provides all these three enhancement services for their publications. In particular, the option to add post-publication data is rarely supported by other publishers. As a contrast, some repositories offer the option of adding commentaries, ranking, trackbacks, or linking publication and research data.

Digital scholarly objects on the Internet such as multimedia materials, data sets and blogs are difficult to find, but their number and importance is steadily growing. Universities and research institutes should therefore assume the responsibility of archiving the digital scholarly output of their organisation in a sustainable way. Repositories have an infrastructure that is very well suited for archiving scholarly output in national libraries or archives. In addition, the disciplinary repositories and the Dataverse Network should be considered.

The main conclusion is that publishers and repositories have the building blocks and the tools, but in general do not use them to create an Enhanced Publication for all three information categories. Publisher and repositories should offer the service and tools to add research data, extra materials and post-publication data to the publications. Researchers should be responsible for the content.

To make it easy for researchers to trace publications and related objects like research data, extra materials or post-publication data, an appropriate infrastructure should be developed. An Enhanced Publication model should support and reflect the relations between a publication and all relevant objects, e.g. data, Web sites, commentaries. In this respect, an Enhanced Publication is developing permanently. The model must therefore be able to add related objects continually, also at a later stage. To handle this complex process, only the OAI-ORE model is sufficient.

The parts of an Enhanced Publication should be carefully selected. Publishers and repositories should set up a checklist for objects of an Enhanced Publication.

Mandatory:
- The object should have a unique global persistent identifier;
- The link must be resolved;
- All objects should have a timestamp;
- The file type should be common, for future use;
- Data sets should have a universal numeric fingerprint;
- 'Cite as' information should be provided;
- Is the quality good enough for preservation?
- Is it legal to publish the object? This question does not only concern copyright.

If known, the following information should be listed with the object:
- Is the object sustainable?
- Does the work have a mark of peer review?
- Is the object machine-readable?
- Is the object freely available?
- Who is the owner?
- Who is responsible?
- Is ranking information available?
- Are there comments available?
- Are there trackbacks available?
- Are there citations to the work? How many times has the material been cited?
- How many times has the material been downloaded?

Finally, the objects should be linked in a meaningful way. It would be helpful for everyone who wants to work with Enhanced Publications to set up general linking models for all publication types like book, dissertation, and article. The links must show what the relation of the object within the Enhanced Publication is. Is it a 'part of', like a chapter of a book, or a 'comment on' the publication? To provide basic semantic interoperability and also to support integration in a large range of different disciplines, ontologies should be used. It is up to the publisher and repository holder to decide how complex the link pattern will be, and if the Enhanced Publication can change over time by adding commentaries after publication.

To keep scholarly publishing efficient and to maintain control over published materials, we need integration of all scientific information, with links between objects. Enhanced Publications can help to integrate scientific information, since they provide explicit links between related objects in order to directly show and support the relations between the objects. This link pattern of Enhanced Publications will help to structure the environment of scholarly publishing, and should therefore make scholarly publishing much more efficient.

Appendix: Identifiers and Identifier Resolution Services

A list with identifiers and identifier resolution services from the eBank Web site[54], accessed March, 2008:

Identifiers

URI, URL, URN[55]

HANDLE. The Handle System is a comprehensive system for assigning, managing, and resolving persistent identifiers, known as 'handles', for digital objects and other resources on the Internet. Handles can be used as Uniform Resource Names (URNs).

DOI. The Digital Object Identifier (DOI) is a system for identifying and exchanging intellectual property in the digital environment.

PURL. A PURL is a Persistent Uniform Resource Locator. Functionally, a PURL is a URL. However, instead of pointing directly to the location of an Internet resource, a PURL points to an intermediate resolution service.

POI. The PURL-based Object Identifier (POI) is a simple specification for resource identifiers based on the PURL system. The use of the POI is closely related to the use of the Open Archives Initiative Protocol for Metadata Harvesting (OAI-PMH) and with the OAI identifier format (OAI-identifiers) used within that protocol. The PURL-based Object Identifier (POI) Andy Powell, Jeff Young, Thom Hickey.
http://www.ukoln.ac.uk/distributed-systems/poi/

The 'info' URI Scheme for Information Assets with Identifiers in Public Namespaces. Herbert Van de Sompel, Tony Hammond, Eamonn Neylon, Stuart L. Weibel.
http://library.caltech.edu/openurl/PubComDocs/Announce/20031003-Announce-infoURI.htm

---

[54] http://www.ukoln.ac.uk/projects/ebank-uk/data-citation/

[55] Missing on the eBank Web site: National Bibliographic Numbers (NBN:URN in use in the Netherlands and Germany).

IVOA Identifiers Version 0.2 (IVOA Working Draft 30 September 2003)
http://www.ivoa.net/Documents/WD/Identifiers/WD-Identifiers-
20030930.html

LSID (I3C) URN Namespace for Life Science Identifiers 4/03/03
http://www.i3c.org/wgr/ta/resources/lsid/docs/LSIDSyntax9-20-02.htm

Lagoze, C., H. Van de Sompel, M. Nelson and S. Warner. 'Specification
and XML Schema for the OAI Identifier Format', June 2002.
http://www.openarchives.org/OAI/2.0/guidelines-oai-identifier.htm

Identifiers for learning objects - a discussion paper Andy Powell.
http://www.ukoln.ac.uk/distributed-systems/lo-identifiers/

Paskin, N., Digital Object Identifiers. Information Services and Use,
22(2/3), 97-112.
http://www.doi.org/topics/020210_CSTI.pdf

NASA Astrophysics Data System Bibliographic Code (bibcodes).
http://adsdoc.harvard.edu/abs_doc/help_pages/data.html

Identifier Resolution Services[56]

Draft Standard for Trial Use ANSI/NISO Z39.88, 'The OpenURL
Framework for Context-Sensitive Services'
http://library.caltech.edu/openurl/Public_Comments.htm

Proposal for a Life Science Identifier Resolution scheme using Web
Services
http://www.i3c.org/wgr/ta/resources/lsid/docs/LSIDResolution.htm

Van de Sompel H, Hochstenbach P. Reference Linking in a Hybrid
Library Environment, Part 1: Frameworks for Linking. D-Lib Magazine,
1999. 5(4).
http://www.dlib.org/dlib/april99/van_de_sompel/04van_de_sompel-
pt1.html

---

[56] Missing on the eBank Web site: DANS resolver (National Dutch Resolver)
http://persistent-identifier.nl

Van de Sompel H, Hochstenbach P, Beit-Arie O (editors). OpenURL Syntax Description. 2000.
http://www.openurl.info/registry/docs/pdf/openurl-01.pdf

Van de Sompel H, Beit-Arie O. Open Linking in the Scholarly Information Environment Using the OpenURL Framework. D-Lib Magazine, 2001. 7(3).
http://www.dlib.org/dlib/march01/vandesompel/03vandesompel.html

Van de Sompel H, Beit-Arie O. Generalizing the OpenURL Framework beyond References to Scholarly Works: the Bison-Futé model. D-Lib Magazine, 2001. 7(7/8).
http://www.dlib.org/dlib/july01/vandesompel/07vandesompel.html

References

Altman, M. (2006). Tools for creating universal numeric fingerprints for data, Version 1.14 (2006-09-11).
http://216.211.131.5/doc/packages/UNF.pdf

Altman, M., Gill, J., & McDonald, M. P. (2003). *Numerical Issues in Statistical Computing for the Social Scientist*. New York: John Wiley and Sons.

Altman, M., & King, G. (2007). A Proposed Standard for the Scholarly Citation of Quantitative Data. *D-Lib Magazine, 13* (3/4).
http://www.dlib.org/dlib/march07/altman/03altman.html

Arms, W. Y., & Larsen, R. L. (2007). *The Future of Scholarly Communication: Building the Infrastructure for Cyberscholarship [Report of a workshop held in Phoenix, Arizona, April 17-19, 2007]* (No. NSF Award # IIS-0645988): Sponsored by the National Science Foundation, And the Joint Information Systems Committee
http://www.sis.pitt.edu/~repwkshop/NSF-JISC-report.pdf

Berners-Lee, T., & Hendler, J. (2001). Publishing on the semantic web: the coming Internet revolution will profoundly affect scientific information. *Nature, 410*, 1023-1024.

Bourne, P. (2005). Will a Biological Database Be Different from a Biological Journal? *PLoS Computational Biology, 1*(3), 179-181.
http://dx.doi.org/10.1371/journal.pcbi.0010034

CIDOC Conceptual Reference Model. (2007). Retrieved 8-3-2009, from http://en.wikipedia.org/wiki/CIDOC_Conceptual_Reference_Model

Doerr, M., Ore, C.-E., & Stead, S. (2007). The CIDOC conceptual reference model: a new standard for knowledge sharing *ACM International Conference Proceeding Series; Vol. 334; Tutorials, posters, panels and industrial contributions at the 26th international conference on Conceptual modeling (Auckland, New Zealand), 83*, 51-56 http://portal.acm.org/citation.cfm?id=1386963

Eichhorn, G., Accomazzi, A., Grant, C. S., Henneken, E. A., Thompson, D. M., Kurtz, M. J., et al. (2007). Connectivity in the Astronomy Digital Library. In S. Ricketts, C. Birdie & E. Isaksson (Eds.), *Library and Information Services in Astronomy V: Common Challenges, Uncommon Solutions* (Vol. 377, pp. 36-42): Astronomical Society of the Pacific. arXiv:cs/0610008v1 [cs.DL].

Fedora Digital Object Relationships - Fedora Repository Release 3.0. (2008). from http://www.fedoracommons.org/documentation/ 3.0/userdocs/digitalobjects/introRelsExt.html

Fink, J. L., & Bourne, P. E. (2007). Reinventing Scholarly Commu-nication for the Electronic Age *CTWatch Quarterly, 3* (3), 26-31. http://www.ctwatch.org/quarterly/articles/2007/08/reinventing-scholarly-communication-for-the-electronic-age/

Foulonneau, M., & André, F. (2007). *The Investigative Study of Standards for Digital Repositories and Related Services*. Amsterdam: Amsterdam University Press.
http://dare.uva.nl/document/93727

Harmsze, F. (2000). *A modular structure for scientific articles in an electronic environment*: Dissertation, University of Amsterdam. An electronic version, including hypertext examples on
http://www.wins.uva.nl/projects/commphys/papers/thesisfh/Front.html

Hunter, J. (2006). Scientific Publication Packages – A selective approach to the communication and archival of scientific output. *Journal of Digital Curation, 1* (1), 3-16.
http://www.ijdc.net/ijdc/article/view/8/7

Kakali, C., Lourdi, I., Stasinopoulou, T., Bountouri, L., Papatheodorou, C., Doerr, M., et al. (2007). Integrating Dublin Core Metadata for Cultural Heritage Collections Using Ontologies. In *International Conference on Dublin Core and Metadata Applications, DC-2007--Singapore Proceedings* (pp. 128-139).
http://www.dcmipubs.org/ojs/index.php/pubs/article/view/16/11

King, G. (2007). An Introduction to the Dataverse Network as an Infrastructure for Data Sharing. *Sociological Methods & Research, 36* (2), 173-199. http://dx.doi.org/10.1177/0049124107306660

Kircz, J. G. (1998). Modularity: The next form of scientific information presentation? *Journal of Documentation, 54* (2), 210-235
http://dx.doi.org/10.1108/EUM0000000007185

Kircz, J. G. (2002). New practices for electronic publishing 2: New forms of the scientific paper. *Learned Publishing, 15* (1), 27-32.
http://dx.doi.org/10.1087/095315102753303652

Lagoze, C., Van de Sompel, H., Johnston, P., Nelson, M., Sanderson, R., & Warner, S. (2008). ORE Specification - Vocabulary [Electronic Version] from http://www.openarchives.org/ore/1.0/vocabulary

Lynch, C. (2007). The Shape of the Scientific Article in the Developing Cyberinfrastructure. *CTWatch Quarterly, 3* (3), 5-10. http://www.ctwatch.org/quarterly/articles/2007/08/the-shape-of-the-scientific-article-in-the-developing-cyberinfrastructure/

Marcondes, C. H. (2005). From scientific communication to public knowledge : the scientific article web published as a knowledge base. In M. Dubrova & J. Engelen (Eds.), *Proceedings International Conference on Electronic Publishing, 9th, ICCC ElPub* (pp. 119-127). Leuven (Belgium).
http://eprints.rclis.org/archive/00005969/

McGuinness, D. L., & van Harmelen, F. (2004). OWL Web Ontology Language: Overview (W3C Recommendation 10 February 2004). Retrieved 8-3-2009, from http://www.w3.org/TR/owl-features/

Place, T. (2008). ORE Experiments presentation at *Open Archives Initiative - Object Reuse and Exchange, UK Open Day, University of Southampton, April 4, 2008.*
http://www.openarchives.org/ore/meetings/Soton/Place-Possible%20ORE%20applications.pdf

Powell, A., Nilsson, M., Naeve, A., Johnston, P., & Baker, T. (2007). DCMI Abstract Model (Recommendation). Retrieved 8-3-2008, from http://dublincore.org/documents/abstract-model/

Sayeed Choudhury, G. (2008). The Virtual Observatory Meets the Library. *Journal of Electronic Publishing, 11*(1).
http://hdl.handle.net/2027/spo.3336451.0011.111

Seeber, F. (2008). Citations in supplementary information are invisible. *Nature, 451* (21 February), 887.

Semantic Web. (2009). Retrieved 20 March 2009, from http://en.wikipedia.org/wiki/Semantic_Web

Seringhaus, M. R., & Gerstein, M. B. (2007). Publishing perishing? Towards tomorrow's information architecture. *Bmc Bioinformatics, 8.* http://www.biomedcentral.com/1471-2105/8/17

Shadbolt, N., Berners-Lee, T., & Hall, W. (2006). The Semantic Web Revisited. *IEEE Intelligent Systems, 21* (3), 96-101. http://portal.acm.org/citation.cfm?id=1386963

Treloar, A., & Groenewegen, D. (2007). ARROW, DART and ARCHER: A Quiver Full of Research Repository and Related Projects. *Ariadne 51* (April 30). http://www.ariadne.ac.uk/issue51/treloar-groenewegen/

Treloar, A., Groenewegen, D., & Harboe-Ree, C. (2007). The Data Curation Continuum. Managing Data Objects in Institutional Repositories *D-Lib Magazine, 13* (9/10).

Van de Sompel, H., & Lagoze, C. (2007). Interoperability for the Discovery, Use, and Re-Use of Units of Scholarly Communication. *CTWatch Quarterly, 3* (3), 32-41. http://www.ctwatch.org/quarterly/articles/2007/08/interoperability-for-the-discovery-use-and-re-use-of-units-of-scholarly-communication/

Van de Sompel, H., Payette, S., Erickson, J., Lagoze, C., & Warner, S. (2004). Rethinking Scholarly Communication: Building the System that Scholars Deserve *D-Lib Magazine, 10* (9). http://www.dlib.org/dlib/september04/vandesompel/09vandesompel.html

Van der Poel, K. G. (2007). *Verkenning van de interesse van wetenschappelijke onderzoekers in WP1-Verrijkte Publicaties en WP2-Collaboratories*. Utrecht: SURF. http://www.surffoundation.nl/download/20070524_Rapport_Verkenning WP12_vdPoel_def.pdf van Horik, R. (2008). Data curation. In K. Weenink, L. Waaijers & K. van Godtsenhoven (Eds.), *A DRIVER's Guide to European Repositories* (pp. 137-138). Amsterdam: Amsterdam University Press.

Wray, A. (2007). *Repositories and Publishers* Paper presented at the OAI-5 Conference, CERN 19 April 2007 from http://indico.cern.ch/materialDisplay.py?contribId=16&sessionId=10&materialId=slides&confId=5710.

PART 2. Object Models and Functionalities

Peter Verhaar

8. Introduction

One of the striking properties of current e-Research projects is unprecedented data intensity. Astronomy, chemistry, geology and archaeology rely on network technologies, automated instruments, image-capture techniques and simulation software. These technologies have a vast impact on the way scientists conduct and disseminate their research. Hey and Treffenden (2003) speak of a 'data deluge' and note that scientists currently *"generate several orders of magnitude more data than has been collected in the whole of human history"* (p.3). For many scientific communities, curation and continued accessibility of such vast quantities of research data poses a challenge. Unfortunately, much data that are produced, often at high costs, also get lost.

Within various disciplines, efforts are made to develop repositories geared especially towards curation of research data. This is compliant with the 2003 Berlin Declaration on Open Access to Knowledge in the Sciences and Humanities, which states that open access contributions can now also include *"original scientific research results, raw data and metadata, source materials, digital representations of pictorial and graphical materials and scholarly multimedia material"*[57]. Examples of projects that focus on stewardship of raw data are the EMBL Nucleotide Sequence Database[58], ARROW (the Australian Research Repositories Online to the World project)[59], and eCrystals, an archive for Crystal Structures created by the Southampton Chemical Crystallography Group and EPSRC UK National Crystallography Service[60]. Funding agencies demanding research projects to secure submission of research data in trusted repositories also stimulate electronic archiving of data.

Open access publishing of scientific data yields a number of advantages, especially in combination with on-line availability of academic manuscripts. When researchers have deposited their raw data, it enables peers to verify the claims. It enables other investigators to re-use data and to compare and combine them with other data, thus generating new research. As additional benefit it will become possible to

---

[57] http://oa.mpg.de/openaccess-berlin/berlindeclaration.html

[58] http://www.ebi.ac.uk/embl/

[59] http://www.arrow.edu.au/

[60] http://ecrystals.chem.soton.ac.uk/

trace the lineage of the products of e-research projects. Research projects normally evolve through stages such as data capture, processing, modelling and interpretation. It would be very helpful if it were possible to highlight the connections between the resources that are produced during different stages in the scientific process.

The current infrastructure for academic communication still focuses on storage and dissemination of individual resources. Libraries and publishers currently use the web primarily to provide access to single articles and monographs. Many academic publishers do not accept other products of e-Research projects, such as databases, video recordings, and web services. At the same time, data repositories rarely link data to the publications in which these data are discussed. The development of a system that can interconnect related scientific web resources is a next step in enhancing the infrastructure for e-Science. This architecture should enable authors to provide access to the results of the full scientific process. On the basis of this improved infrastructure, new services can be built that enable researchers to reuse existing results and to exchange scientific and scholarly resources across institutions, disciplines and repositories.

In the last few years, various studies have investigated the possibility to intertwine distributed e-Research products. Hunter (2007) envisions the creation of 'Scientific Publication Packages', which are described as 'compound digital objects that encapsulate and relate the raw data to its derived products, publications and the associated contextual, provenance and administrative metadata' (p.33). Similarly, the Object Reuse and Exchange (OAI-ORE) working group has developed standards for the description and exchange of aggregations of Web resources.

In this publication we will identify the requirements for storing and managing Enhanced Publications within the DRIVER infrastructure. Firstly a description of the term 'Enhanced Publication' is given. Then we review the most important technical and functional requirements, followed by recommendations for the implementation of Enhanced Publications. On the basis of these requirements and recommendations, a data model has been developed. Finally, we will provide recommendations for a serialisation of this data model in XML.

We will propose a generic model for storage and management of Enhanced Publications, preparing ground for the specification requirements for a new DRIVER service, Active Information Discovery, in which the concept of Enhanced Publications is demonstrated. We will also ensure that the model that is proposed in this report will comply with more encompassing vision on compound digital objects.

The model that is discussed in this book may be adopted by other projects that intend to publish textual documents in combination with related resources. It should be emphasised, however, that here we offer only a very broad perspective on this topic. Many details of the implementation are still to be filled in. This qualification of the scope is inevitable, since issues related to terminology, data reuse, methodology and certification will often be specific to a particular discipline, or even to a particular research institute or laboratory. The aim is to formulate guidelines that enable system developers to set up the general outline of a technical infrastructure for Enhanced Publications. The model that is proposed is also intended to stimulate further discussion on this relatively new phenomenon in academic communication.

9.   Definitions and Principles

The limitations of traditional publishing as for its capacity to incorporate the results from the entire scientific discovery process gave an impetus to the enhancement of publications. Although large data sets may be generated, an academic text can normally present the research data in a condensed form only. Cheung et al. (2008) note that scientific publications *"inadequately represent the earlier stages [of the scientific process] that involve the capture, analysis, modelling and interpretation of primary scientific data"* (p.1). This limitation has become problematic in recent years since many scientific disciplines are currently producing digital data at highly prodigious rates and in ever growing quantities. Borgman (2007) argues that the *"predicted data deluge is already a reality in many fields"* (p.113).

Fortunately, the data that are produced are increasingly stored in trusted data repositories. The aim of such data curation is to ensure that scholarly and scientific materials can be preserved and reused. A shortcoming in the current infrastructure for academic communication is that these datasets are usually not connected to the scientific publications in which they are discussed[61]. Enhanced Publications are created with the aim of bridging this imminent gap between the contents of institutional repositories and the contents of data repositories. They ultimately will enable agents to access the complete results of academic studies, and to trace the workflow in research projects.

Enhanced Publications are envisioned as compound digital objects, which can combine heterogeneous but related web resources. The basis of this compound object is the traditional academic publication. This refers to a textual resource with original work, which is intended for reading by human beings, and which puts forward certain academic claims. Following the *Investigative Study of Standards for Digital Repositories and Related Services*, a study carried out as part of the DRIVER project, we will use the term 'ePrint'. Foulonneau and André define it as an *"electronic version of academic research paper"* (p.109). An ePrint is understood as a scholarly work, which contains an

---

[61] A notable exception is the CDS info hub in astronomy: http://cdsweb.u-strasbg.fr/

interpretation or an analysis of certain primary data, or of a derivation from these materials. Examples of ePrints include dissertations, journal articles, working papers, book chapters or reports.

In the humanities and in the social sciences textual materials such as electronic transcriptions or e-Books frequently are object of academic research. When these are used as primary data in a study, they are not considered to be ePrints, as an ePrint is assumed to be a text that discusses the outcome of an investigation of such source materials. In a growing number of disciplines non-textual resources will be accepted as academic publications. Activities such as the creation of an authoritative database, or the determination of a crystal structure can be subject to academic rewards. Nevertheless, we will restrict ourselves to publications in the traditional meaning of the word.

Enhancing a publication involves adding resources to this ePrint. These can be the resources that have been produced or consulted during the creation of the text. In general they support, justify, illustrate or clarify the scientific claims that are put forward in a publication. An academic manuscript is normally stored in an institutional repository and other components, potentially from other repositories, are added to this publication as part of the workflow in scientific research projects.

An example of an Enhanced Publication is an ePrint combined with a metadata record. Such a metadata record can be made available as an individual resource, for instance, as an XML stream that is returned as the result of an OAI-PMH *getRecord* request. ePrints usually will be described using descriptive or bibliographic metadata. Examples of descriptive metadata standards are the Metadata Object Description Schema (MODS), Qualified Dublin Core (QDC) and Machine Readable Cataloguing (MARC).

A second type of entity that can be connected to the ePrint is data. OECD, in its *Recommendation of the Council concerning Access to Research Data from Public Funding*, describes research data as *"factual records (numerical scores, textual records, images and sounds) used as primary sources for scientific research, and that are commonly accepted in the scientific community as necessary to validate research findings"*[62].

---

[62] http://webdomino1.oecd.org/horizontal/oecdacts.nsf/Display/?OpenDocument

The term 'data' may refer to any of the following types of objects:

- Data collections containing, for instance, the results of experiments, measurements performed by technical instruments or the results of surveys;
- Data visualisations, such as graphs, diagrams, tables, or 3D models;
- Machine-readable chemical structures;
- Multimedia files such as images, video files or audio recordings;
- Mathematical formulae, possibly expressed in MathXML, or algorithms;
- Text documents that are part of a corpus created for research purposes;
- Software, which may be provided as source code, or implemented as web services;
- Commentaries and annotations made by agents who have consulted digital objects. Notes on why certain components are relevant or valuable for a specific line of research can be very useful for other academics;
- Specifications of instruments or other hardware;
- Digital certificates for research instruments.

Such related data objects may also be described in metadata records. Research data can be described on the basis of the Data Documentation Initiative (DDI), which is a highly expressive standard that can be used to describe the coverage of a study and the methodologies that were used. Preservation metadata capture information that is needed to ensure the long-term curation of information resources. PREMIS is the most widely accepted standard. Technical metadata standards such as NISO/MIX provide a format for storing technical aspects of resources. An advanced example of an Enhanced Publication may thus consist of a combination of an ePrint, metadata for this ePrint, data objects, and metadata for these data objects.

In conclusion, Enhanced Publications can be defined as compound digital objects, which combine ePrints with one or more metadata records, one or more data resources, or any combination of these. Since the DRIVER project focuses on academic publications in the traditional sense, it is assumed here that an Enhanced Publication must minimally include one ePrint.

10. Requirements and Recommendations

10.1 Structure of Enhanced Publications

In Chapter 9, it is explained that Enhanced Publications are compound digital objects that combine ePrints, research data and metadata. The creation of such scholarly packages should eventually become part of the natural working environment of scientists. Some simple tools should be developed that enable academics to archive their data and the descriptions of these data in a digital repository shortly after their creation. Seringhaus and Gerstein (2007) express a similar need. They argue that new information architecture should be developed which must *"ensure that every author is able to archive pre-prints, host supplementary data, and make their findings available in digital format"*.

It is advisable to make sure that manuscripts and research data that are deposited in repositories also become part of the web architecture. This implies that all these objects will be available as web resources that can be referenced via a URI. A recommended practice would be to associate globally unique and persistent identifiers with each of these resources. Foulonneau and André (2008) provide an overview of the identifiers that are currently in use within various scientific communities. When scientists publish and share multiple heterogeneous resources through the web, there should be a framework that enables scientists to specify which resources belong together. Enhanced Publications are produced precisely for this purpose. They can be understood as envelopes, or as enumerations that provide an overview of which ePrints, research data and metadata are published in conjunction.

It is advisable to separate the identification of a resource from its localisation through resolvers that are capable of translating the identifier to a certain bit stream that can be accessed at a specific network location. Such a resolver should also be able to adapt in the situation where one digital object is moved from one repository to the other. This provision is needed to ensure that references to the components of the Enhanced Publication are stable and reliable.

The components of an Enhanced Publication do not necessarily have to be stored in a single repository. They may be distributed over different network locations. When publications are enhanced with resources that are maintained at various locations, this may give rise to legal issues. Authors of Enhanced Publications whose components span multiple institutions are advised to ensure that they also have permission to aggregate these different resources. The architecture for Enhanced Publications should support references not only to resources in their entirety, but under certain conditions also to specific locations within these resources. For instance, it should be possible to point to a specific table or even to a specific record or group of records within a database.

Requirement 1
It must be possible at any moment to specify the component parts of an Enhanced Publication.

An Enhanced Publication basically creates a new layer on top of existing resources. It functions as an overlay that clarifies the structure of a coherent collection of resources. Normally, the resources that are aggregated also exist as independent information units outside of the context of the compound object, which means that they can also be used in other environments. This is important, since there is rarely a strictly one-to-one relationship between, for instance, an ePrint and an e-research object. An ePrint may use various databases, and one database may have inspired various academic texts.

To stimulate the usage of Enhanced Publications in academic communication, it is essential to ensure that they can be cited. For this reason, the institution that publishes an Enhanced Publication must make it available as a web resource and associate an identifier with it. Ideally, this identifier should be globally unique and persistent. It should be possible to resolve this identifier to a representation of the Enhanced Publication.

Requirement 2
Both the Enhanced Publication and its components must be available as web resources that can be referenced via URIs.

10.2   Compound Objects

Kahn and Wilensky (2006) distinguish elemental and composite digital objects. Research data are often available as elemental or atomic web resources. This means that they can be represented as a single bit stream at a single network location. Several atomic resources may be clustered into a larger compound object. Such compound data sets may consist of multiple data files and of multiple metadata records. It should also be possible to add such compound objects to the publication. One Enhanced Publication may also wholly aggregate a second Enhanced Publication. Such a nested structure may occur in the case of e-theses that consist of parts that are also available as separate resources, such as journal articles or pre-publications. These texts may in turn aggregate other resources such as images, video files, audio recordings, data sets or metadata records. Enhanced Publications can thus be highly complex and multi-tiered objects.

> *Requirement 3*
> **It must be possible to add compound digital objects to the publication.**

10.3   Versioning

Enhanced Publications are potentially dynamic resources. When they contain data from research projects that are still in progress, resources may be added, updated or even removed on a regular basis. Such alterations potentially invalidate certain applications that were based on this Enhanced Publication. For this reason, agents who use an Enhanced Publication must refer to specific versions of the compound object. The versioning issue is also important as to individual components. Research data can be dynamic since, for instance, data sets can grow, multimedia files can be modified and software specifications may be altered. Similarly, ePrints may also be modified in the course of a project. Individual repository managers must answer the question what qualifies as a new version. The Version Identification Framework (VIF)[63], which was funded by JISC, provides useful documentation on the issue of versioning. In this framework, a version is defined as "*a digital object, in whatever format, that exists in time and place and has*

---

[63] Website: http://www.lse.ac.uk/library/vif/

a context within a larger body of work". Versions can be identified by recording the date of the last modification, version identification, or textual description of the version.

Requirement 4
It must be possible to keep track of the different versions of both the Enhanced Publication as a whole, and of its constituent parts.

10.4 Basic Properties

To enable service providers to develop applications on the basis of Enhanced Publications a number of key properties of the various resources in the Enhanced Publication should be described. To make Enhanced Publications interoperable, these properties should be described using a standardised and controlled vocabulary as much as possible. Chapter 12 will propose a number of vocabularies that can be used.

The following attributes will be relevant in the majority of cases:
- Each component should be typed semantically to make it clear what kind of resource is being referred to;
- ePrints can have a title;
- For atomic or compound datasets, a brief description may be given. It is advisable to provide a title, which makes it explicit that these particular resources are data objects;
- For Enhanced Publications as a whole, it will be useful to record the date of the last modification. In the case of newly created publications, this date will coincide with the date of creation;
- Since different applications are mostly needed to process or to present the various resources that are aggregated, it will be necessary to describe the technical format of the resource. Media types and media formats can be recorded using the IANA registered list of Internet Media Types. Recording this aspect is optional since the precise media type may not always be known beforehand. This may be the case for web resources that are available in different representations. Such resources can be resolved to a certain media type at the moment of request through the process of content negotiation;

- The MIME type can also be specified for metadata. Since there are many metadata vocabularies that have not yet been acknowledged as an IANA Media Type, it will be more useful to record the namespace of the metadata schema.

E-science projects are increasingly collaborative and interdisciplinary processes. To be able to trace individual contributions, authorships on all levels of the Enhanced Publication must be recorded. Capturing the provenance may also help clients to establish the trustworthiness of the resource. A clear distinction must be made between the author of the Enhanced Publication and the authors of its component parts. Authors of ePrints and data resources are the agents who are responsible for their intellectual contents. The author of the Enhanced Publication as a whole is the agent who has decided to combine the various resources into a single compound object. Evidently, authorship of the Enhanced Publication does not automatically imply authorship of associated ePrints or associated data sets.

10.5 Long-term Preservation

A growing number of institutions are developing repositories that aim to preserve digital content for future generations. Notable initiatives are the e-Depot of the Dutch National Library and the NESTOR and KOPAL projects, which were initiated by the German National Library and the University and State Library of Göttingen. Such institutions mostly employ a combination of techniques to guarantee longevity, including migration, which involves transferring bits from one format or medium to another, and emulation. This technique involves an imitation of the functionality of a certain obsolete program or operating system to preserve the usability of a digital resource (Lorie, 2001). It must be possible to harvest the document that serialises the Enhanced

Publication from local repositories and to ingest it into digital archiving systems.

Institutions responsible for the long-term accessibility and usability may choose to harvest and preserve the individual parts of the Enhanced Publication as well. For this reason, it must be possible to harvest representations of the web resources that are referred to in the scientific package. As explained earlier, the structure of an Enhanced Publication is not always fixed. This is especially the case for publications that are created for research projects that have not yet been completed. Consequently, it may be difficult to decide for repository managers or for owners of the long-term preservation archives (LTP Archives) when exactly the publication should be archived. In the case of the more dynamic publications, it is especially important to capture versioning information. Long term archives can leverage this information by deciding to preserve one specific version of the Enhanced Publication, instead of having to wait until the entire Enhanced Publication is complete. The key data that are recommended in Paragraph 10.4 also help managers of LTP archives to generate appropriate preservation metadata for the various objects whose long term accessibility need to be ensured.

Requirement 7
It must be possible to secure the long-term preservation of Enhanced Publications.

10.6   Relations

Whereas repositories currently focus mostly on storing individual digital objects, one should recognise that there are often strong links between the various resources that can be found in different data repositories or institutional repositories. A crystal X-ray structure determination in a data repository, for instance, may have lead to further studies, the results of which are stored elsewhere. Resources can be related both to atomic objects and to compound objects. It is essential in the data model for Enhanced Publications that these relations can be stated explicitly. Such descriptions of the links between the resources help to clarify the reasons why these resources were added to the collection. This will enable authors of Enhanced Publications to present these resources in a coherent framework. Relations between the various component parts need to be described and classified using a standard and generic vocabulary as much as possible.

An overview of the most common kinds of relations that occur is provided here:

- *Containment relations.* Two resources are considered to be connected through a containment relation if one unit is included physically or logically within another unit. This is a very common kind of relation, as it occurs each time a number of resources are grouped or clustered into a larger unit. Examples include e-theses that consist of different chapters, or directory structures that are published in their entirety as Enhanced Publications. Containment relations can always be represented visually by means of a tree diagram.

- *Sequential relations.* In certain situations, it may be necessary to record the order in which resources need to be consulted. This is the case, for instance, if the separate components of a monograph or an article are included as individual parts. The aim of sequential relations is to establish a reading path within a session.

- *Versioning information.* It is often necessary to maintain different versions of a certain resource. Specific relater terms may be used to provide information on the relations between such different versions.

- *Lineage relations.* Lineage relations provide information on the order in which research data are produced. Hunter (*2006*) explains that the lineage of data production refers to the *"chain (or pipeline) of processing steps used to generate scientific data and derived products"* (p. 37). When such relations are made explicit, it enables peers to trace the various stages of the scientific process.

- *Manifestations.* Web resources are often available in different technical formats. For instance, an article may be available both as an HTML file and as a PDF document. Similarly, archive copies of images are often stored in TIFF or JPEG2000 format, in addition to the presentation copies in JPG or GIF format. The various manifestations may be clustered within an aggregation that brings these various formats together.

- *Bibliographic citations.* Academic publications usually contain many bibliographic references to other publications. References can be both to resources that are stored in a trusted repository and to resources that are stored at other types of locations. The decision on whether a link to such external and less reliable sources is allowed is for individual repository managers to make.

Relations can be unidirectional and bidirectional. Many ontologies define only unidirectional relations. This implies that, if resource A has a relation with resource B, the inverse relation cannot be assumed automatically. If that inverse relation can exist, it mostly needs to be expressed explicitly, by using an antonym of the first term. For example, if resource A contains resource B, this can be expressed by using the term 'hasPart'. The inverse relation can be expressed explicitly by using the term 'isPartOf'. Defining such unidirectional relations may introduce a degree of redundancy, and it may certainly not always be feasible, especially when resources are distributed over many repositories. However, when it is applied, it will have the effect that each resource carries explicit information about the relations that it is involved in. It will also ensure that web resources can be viewed both individually and as part of an Enhanced Publication. This increases the flexibility of the constituent parts of the Enhanced Publication.

10.7 Discovery

Enhanced Publications must be usable and visible in largely the same systems that are used to store, index and retrieve atomic digital objects. Their contents must be accessible to services that leverage repository content such as web crawlers, citation analysis tools, harvesters and data mining applications. Individual agents who may be interested in using the compound publication must be enabled to discover them. This means, more concretely, that they should have the possibility to learn about their existence.

Processes of locating, retrieving and promulgating Enhanced Publications can be based on a wide range of techniques, including site maps, syndication or OAI-PMH. The question of which technique is the most relevant largely depends on the requirements of the discovering agent. Evidently, a technique such as OAI-PMH will only be relevant if service providers have the tools that are needed to perform OAI-PMH based harvests.

Requirement 9
Institutions that offer access to Enhanced Publications must make sure that they can be discovered.

10.8   OAI-ORE

Since it is assumed in this report that OAI-ORE will be established as the de facto standard for capturing and exchanging information on generic compound objects, institutions should take measures to ensure that Enhanced Publications are available as documents based on the OAI-ORE model. OAI-ORE provides a way to combine disparate web resources into a single unit. As is explained in Van de Sompel (2007), a central aim of OAI-ORE is *"to develop standardised, interoperable, and machine-readable mechanisms to express compound object information on the web"* [64]. It provides a framework for capturing machine-readable descriptions of compound objects through a mechanism that is known as named graphs. More specific information on OAI-ORE is provided in Chapter 3.5. The requirement that Enhanced Publications must be available as documents based on the OAI-ORE model does not imply any subsequent prescriptions for the internal storage of the resource. An Enhanced Publication is essentially information about a collection of resources, and such data may be stored, for instance, in relational databases, or in other XML formats such as MPEG21-DIDL or METS.

Requirement 10
Institutions that provide access to Enhanced Publications must ensure that these are available as documents based on the OAI-ORE model.

---

[64] http://www.openarchives.org/ore/documents/CompoundObjects-200705.html

11. Data Model

The previous chapter has identified a number of functional and technical requirements for the storage and management of Enhanced Publications. This chapter will present an abstract model that can represent these requirements. This data model may be the basis for the further development of the infrastructure for compound objects within the DRIVER infrastructure.

A starting point for the content model is the observation that Enhanced Publications are compound digital objects, which combine ePrints with one or more data resources, one or more metadata records, or any combination of these. We will assume that an Enhanced Publication must minimally include one ePrint. This term has been defined in Chapter 9. When a data object is combined with one or more metadata records, or with one or more other data objects, the resulting package is referred to as a compound dataset. Enhanced Publications thus can include five types of entities:

- ePrints;
- Data objects;
- Metadata;
- Compound datasets;
- Enhanced Publications.

The first two types of entities are atomic objects and the latter two entities are compound in nature, which means that they aggregate other atomic objects.

Advanced discovery services may require that some key metadata are present for the various resources that are aggregated. Therefore, it must be possible to record a number of basic properties, not only for all digital objects that are included but also for the Enhanced Publication in its entirety. In accordance with the Kahn and Wilensky architecture for distributed digital object services (2006) a digital object is understood as *"an instance of an abstract type that has two components, data and key-metadata"* whereby the *"key-metadata includes a handle, i.e. an identifier globally unique to the digital object"* (p.117).

The properties that are likely to be relevant in the most common situations have been listed in Chapter 10. It should be noted that it is not mandatory to implement all the attributes that have been mentioned. They must be considered optional, with the possible exception of the identifier. Moreover, repository managers may also choose to include other types and properties if they are considered necessary. Figure 9 offers a first overview of the five entities and their key properties.

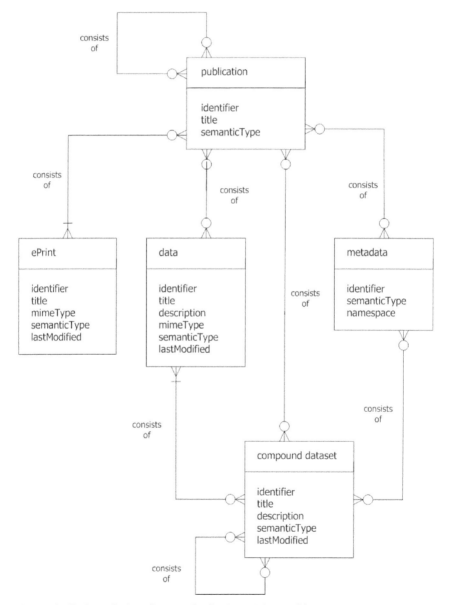

Figure 9. Entity-relation diagram for basic entities and key properties

The model that is presented in Figure 9 is still incomplete, as there are three additional requirements that need to be represented. Firstly, it must be possible to keep track of the different versions of both the Enhanced Publication as a whole, and of its constituent parts. Secondly, it must be possible to capture the provenance of the Enhanced Publication and of the various resources that it combines. All the entities that are listed in Figure 9 can be associated with an agent who is responsible for its existence. This agent can be an individual, an institution or perhaps a fully automated application. A third requirement is that it must be possible to describe relations between resources. These three additional requirements apply to all the entities that are given in Figure 9.

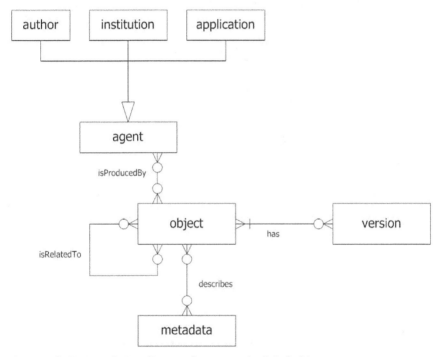

Figure 10. Entity-relation diagram for a generic digital object

To be able to visualise these additional requirements in an orderly fashion, it has been decided to extend the model with the generic notion of a digital object. This abstract object may be either atomic or compound in nature. Figure 10 visualises the observations that digital objects can be produced by zero or more authors, that they can be related to zero or more other objects, and that they can appear in one or more versions.

The diagram also indicates that these digital objects can be described by metadata records, and that these objects may have been produced by three types of agents, namely individual authors, institutions, or automated applications. For the sake of clarity, all attributes have been omitted from this diagram.

To finalise the data model, it must be indicated that the abstract data object may occur in two basic types. It may be either an atomic object or a compound object. The atomic object may be included fully as a bit stream, or it may be included in the form of a URI reference. Compound objects are created by combining one or more atomic objects. This diagram also states that publications and compound datasets are specific instances of compound objects.

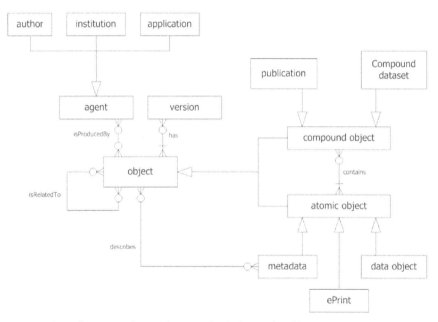

Figure 11. Full entity-relation diagram for Enhanced Publications

In conclusion, the model that is presented in Figure 11 captures the most important requirements for the storage and management of Enhanced Publications. It also indicates the global manner in which Enhanced Publications must ultimately manifest themselves within the Driver infrastructure. Since an Enhanced Publication is essentially a specific instance of the more general notion 'compound object', they must be supported as special instances of the Compound Object data

116

model[65]. The Compound Object Model Specification discusses the modelling abstractions that are required to describe document models of any Digital Library application domain. The Compound Object data model that has been developed also inspires the implementation of Content Services, which are capable of supporting efficient storage and search of Driver Compound Objects.

Such a model can be applied to express the basic requirements for Enhanced Publications. It describes compound objects as sets of digital objects that are associated on the basis of relationships. The low-level model provides the minimal set of primitives required to design efficient compound object digital libraries. It supports the notions of Type, Set and Object. Types define the abstract structure and the operators of the Object entities, and they can be instantiated as Sets, which are the concrete types of the objects they contain. Sets can be of three main types: Atom Type, Structure Type and Relation Type. To construct instances of Enhanced Publications, it is firstly necessary to define the resources that we referred to as 'atomic' resources. More precisely, this refers to the entities that in Figure 11 are labelled 'ePrint', 'metadata object' and 'data object'. This must be followed by an instantiation of relative sets. Once these atomic objects are defined, they can used to define Relationship types, which are 'dependent types'. This means that their creation depends on two existing, i.e. created, Sets. A second mechanism to construct dependent types are the so-called Union types, of the form "Union(A1,...Ak)". They can be used to create Sets whose objects belong to any of the Sets A1, ...,Ak. The TDL expression exemplify how a compound object can be created by combining ePrints with data objects: Set compoundObjects = create Union(ePrints, dataObjects).

Again, these dependent types must be followed by an instantiation of the relative sets. Enhanced Publications can be constructed by defining atomic types, and by subsequently defining dependent types that combine these atomic types into larger units. The Enhanced Publication model thus clearly complies with the basic vision on compound digital objects.

---

[65] *D8.1. Compound Object Model Specification.* The model is also discussed in *Typed Compound Object Models for Digital Library Repository Systems*, Leonardo Candela, Donatella Castelli, Paolo Manghi, Marko Mikulicic, Pasquale Pagano. ISTI Technical Report 2008-TR-023.

12. Vocabularies

One of the requirements that were identified in Chapter 10 is that it must be possible to record key metadata of digital objects. To make Enhanced Publications semantically interoperable, the properties that were mentioned must be described using a standardised and controlled vocabulary as much as possible. This section will propose a number of vocabularies that can be used in this context.

The DCMI Type Vocabulary provides a number of terms that may be used to describe the semantic type.

Value URI	Label
http://purl.org/dc/dcmitype/Dataset	Dataset
http://purl.org/dc/dcmitype/Event	Event
http://purl.org/dc/dcmitype/Image	Image
http://purl.org/dc/dcmitype/InteractiveResource	InteractiveResource
http://purl.org/dc/dcmitype/MovingImage	MovingImage
http://purl.org/dc/dcmitype/Software	Software
http://purl.org/dc/dcmitype/Sound	Sound
http://purl.org/dc/dcmitype/Text	Text

ePrints may be classified as such using the term 'Text'. A more specific classification of the semantic type of ePrints can be provided on the basis of the vocabulary set that has been compiled for the info:eu-repo namespace. A full overview can be found at the following address: http://info-uri.info/registry/OAIHandler?verb= GetRecord&metadataPrefix=reg &identifier=info:eu-repo/

The ePrints Application Profile[66] defines a simple vocabulary to describe access rights. It prescribes terms such as 'Open Access', 'Restricted Access' and 'Closed Access'.

Containments relations can be stated explicitly by making use of 'isPartOf' and 'hasPart' from the Dublin Core Metadata Initiative.

---

[66] Website:
http://www.ukoln.ac.uk/repositories/digirep/index/Eprints_Application_Profile

Value URI	Label
http://purl.org/dc/terms/isPartOf	isPartOf
http://purl.org/dc/terms/hasPart	hasPart

The Dublin Core Metadata Initiative also provides a vocabulary that can be used to record the relation between different versions.

Value URI	Label
http://purl.org/dc/terms/isVersionOf	isVersionOf
http://purl.org/dc/terms/hasVersion	hasVersion
http://purl.org/dc/terms/isReplacedBy	isReplacedBy
http://purl.org/dc/terms/Replaces	Replaces

Separate digital manifestations can be connected as follows:

Value URI	Label
http://purl.org/dc/terms/isFormatOf	isFormatOf
http://purl.org/dc/terms/hasFormat	hasFormat

Bibliographic references in the publication can be made explicit by using 'References' from the Dublin Core Terms Namespace, and 'Is Referenced By' for the inverse relation.

Value URI	Label
http://purl.org/dc/terms/references	References
http://purl.org/dc/terms/isReferencedBy	Is Referenced By

To describe lineage relations, the ABC Model that is developed by Hunter and Lagoze (2001) may be used. The model contains terms such as 'precedes', 'follows', 'contains', 'isSubEventOf', 'phaseOf', 'involves', 'usesTool', 'hasResult', 'hasAction' and 'hasPresence'.

Academic work is increasingly made public under a Creative Commons licence[67]. Usage rights may be described using the dc:rights property.

Value URI	Label
http://purl.org/dc/elements/1.1/rights	Rights

---

[67] http://creativecommons.org/licenses/by-nc-sa/2.0/

13. Recommendation for Serialisation

This chapter will explain how the OAI-ORE data model can be applied to exchange information about Enhanced Publications. Such guidelines are needed, since the OAI-ORE effort does not limit itself to connecting publications with data sets. It offers a broad framework for compound digital objects in general. The OAI-ORE vocabulary can be used in RDF statements to specify that a collection of URI-identified resources together form a compound object. The advantage of OAI-ORE is that it can be adopted to encapsulate distributed resources. OAI-ORE focuses on resources, and not on repositories.

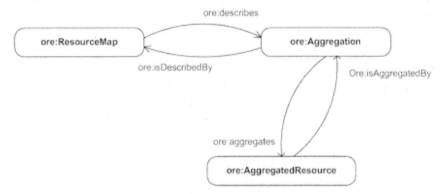

Figure 12. Basics of the OAI-ORE model

The OAI-ORE data model distinguishes three entities:

1. The 'Aggregation' is a collection of web resources. Individually, these are referred to as 'Aggregated Resources'.
2. A 'Resource Map' is an entity that contains a description of an 'Aggregation'. There are five properties that can relate these entities. The connection between the Resource Map and the Aggregation can be established using 'describes' and its inverse relation 'isDescribedBy'. An aggregated resource becomes part of an enumeration of resources if the resource map asserts the 'aggregates' relation between this resource and the aggregation. The link from an Aggregated Resource to the Aggregation can be expressed using 'isAggregatedBy'.
3. There is also the property 'similarTo' to denote the fact that two resources are identical.

121

In Chapter 9 it is explained that an Enhanced Publication is headed by an ePrint, and that enhancements can be added to this text in the form of research data, metadata records, compound datasets and other Enhanced Publications. The data model for Enhanced Publications in the report thus bears a strong similarity to the OAI-ORE abstract data model. The Publication entity may be mapped to the Aggregation and the enhancements correspond to the Aggregated Resources. The Resource Map is the document through which the Enhanced Publication may be accessed. Lagoze and Van de Sompel (2007) explain that Resource Maps are used *"to expose to harvesting clients the compound objects that they provide access to",* amongst other things. The Resource Map thus references the fully Enhanced Publication. The Aggregation has an identifier that is derived from the URI of the Resource Map. A Resource Map always describes only one Aggregation, but an Aggregation may be described by more than one Resource Map. One Aggregated Resource can also be part of more than one Aggregation.

To be able to express the key metadata for the various resources, the attributes that were mentioned in Chapter 10 must be mapped to terms that can be used as properties in RDF statements. Following the OAI-ORE documentation, this report will use vocabulary from the Dublin Core Metadata Element Set, the DCMI Metadata Terms and the Resource Description Framework in a recommended concordance.

Attributes	Property
identifier	dc:identifier
title	dc:title
description	dc:description
author	dc:creator
semanticType	rdf:type
versionIdentification	dc:hasVersion
versionDate	dcterms:modified
versionDescription	dc:description
mimeType	dc:format
namespace	dcterms:conformsTo
lastModified	dcterms:modified

The guidelines that have been presented so far will be illustrated using two examples. The first sample-Enhanced Publication is taken from the

Network of European Economists Online (NEEO) project, which is coordinated at the University of Tilburg. The bibliographic details of this publication have been adapted slightly for the sake of clarity. It is a compound object that consists of an ePrint, a metadata record in MODS, and a dataset. Figure 13 indicates how information about such a constellation can be described using the OAI-ORE vocabulary.

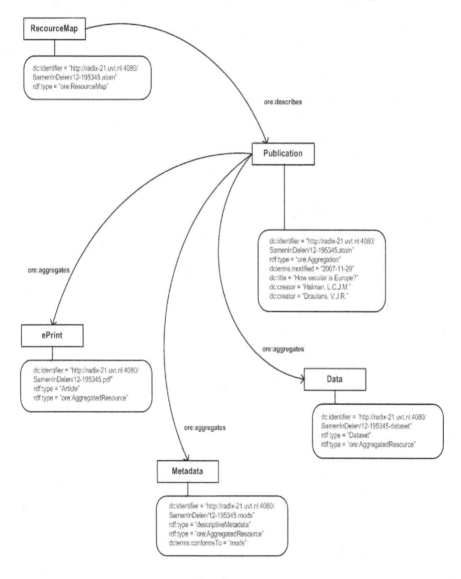

Figure 13. Serialisation of an Enhanced Publication (Example 1)

The listing below illustrates how this information can be expressed using RDF/XML.

```
<?xml version="1.0" encoding="UTF-8"?>
<rdf:RDF xmlns:rdf="http://www.w3.org/1999/02/22-rdf-syntax-ns#"
xmlns:xs="http://www.w3.org/2001/XMLSchema"
xmlns:rdfs="http://www.w3.org/2000/01/rdf-schema#"
xmlns:foaf="http://xmlns.com/foaf/0.1/"
xmlns:dc="http://purl.org/dc/elements/1.1/"
xmlns:dcterms="http://purl.org/dc/terms/"
xmlns:ore="http://www.openarchives.org/ore/terms/"
xmlns:xhtml="http://www.w3.org/1999/xhtml">

<rdf:Description rdf:about="http://radix-21.uvt.nl:4080/
        SamenInDelen/listOfItems.atom">
<rdf:type rdf:resource="http://www.openarchives.org/ore
        /terms/ResourceMap"/>
<ore:describes rdf:resource="http://radix-21.uvt.nl:4080/
        SamenInDelen/12-195345"/>
</rdf:Description>

<rdf:Description rdf:about="http://radix-21.uvt.nl:4080/
        SamenInDelen/12-195345">
<rdf:type rdf:resource="http://www.openarchives.org/ore/terms/
        Aggregation"/>
<dcterms:modified>2007-11-29T09:40:01Z</dcterms:modified>
<ore:aggregates rdf:resource="http://radix-21.uvt.nl:4080/
        SamenInDelen/12-195345.mods"/>
<ore:aggregates rdf:resource="http://radix-21.uvt.nl:4080/
        SamenInDelen/12-195345-dataset"/>
</rdf:Description>

<rdf:Description rdf:about="http://drcwww.uvt.nl/~place/
        SamenInDelen/12-195345-eft.doc">
<rdf:type rdf:resource="http://www.openarchives.org/ore/terms/
        AggregatedResource"/>
<rdf:type rdf:resource="info:eu-repo/semantics/article"/>
<dc:title>How secular is Europe?</dc:title>
<dc:creator>Halman, L.C.J.M.</dc:creator>
<dc:creator>Draulans, V.J.R.</dc:creator>
</rdf:Description>
<rdf:Description rdf:about="http://radix-21.uvt.nl:4080/
        SamenInDelen/12-195345.mods">
<rdf:type rdf:resource="http://www.openarchives.org/ore/terms/
        AggregatedResource"/>
<rdf:type rdf:resource="info:eu-repo/semantics/
        descriptiveMetadata"/>
<dcterms:conformsTo>mods</dcterms:conformsTo>
</rdf:Description>
<rdf:Description rdf:about="http://radix-21.uvt.nl:4080/
        SamenInDelen/12-195345-dataset">
<rdf:type rdf:resource="http://www.openarchives.org/ore/terms/
        AggregatedResource"/>
<rdf:type rdf:resource="http://purl.org/dc/dcmitype/Dataset"/>
</rdf:Description>
</rdf:RDF>
```

The OAI-ORE documentation contains guidelines for serialisations of the model in RDF/XML and in ATOM. A serialisation has the advantage that, in the case of research projects that are still in progress, clients can be notified of new additions through a feed reader. Details of the serialisations in ATOM and RDF/XML can be found in Van de Sompel et al. (2008).

In more advanced compound objects one of the aggregated resources may be another Enhanced Publication, which is published separately. This may occur when a publication is a collection of texts written by various authors. A layered or nested structure may also be necessary in the case of large e-theses. When sizeable quantities of digital data are accumulated for different chapters, it can be effective to disaggregate the complete e-theses into smaller units. Figure 14 depicts an example in which one chapter of an e-thesis is available as a separate compound object. In that situation, aggregated chapters can be enhanced with specific metadata records. The e-thesis aggregates its first chapter by pointing to the URI of the Chapter 1 Aggregation. When this URI is de-referenced, it should produce the Resource Map of the first chapter.

Subject to debate is the question whether or not the Resource Map should explicitly specify all the manifestations that are available for digital objects. An ePrint, for instance, may be available as a PDF file, a DOC file, a simple text file or an HTML page. If such manifestations all need to be mentioned in the resource map, it will be useful to cluster them in an aggregation. In FRBR terminology, this aggregation may be said to function as an "Expression" which can be embodied in different 'Manifestations', which may each appear as Aggregated Resources within this aggregation. This solution has the advantage that it is made very clear which digital objects (bit streams) actually exist for the resource. This way, users can intentionally select one particular manifestation. An alternative solution would be to leverage the Web Architecture, and to simply incorporate the URI of the expression as an Aggregated Resource. The various manifestations then can be reached through the process of Content Negotiation, at the moment when the URI is de-referenced. Such a solution would make the Resource Map more economic. A disadvantage, however, is that it may not always be predictable for clients which kind of manifestation they will actually receive, since this latter question will be determined by comparing the objects that are available in the repository with the objects that the client can accept. Figure 14 illustrates the first method of dealing with manifestations.

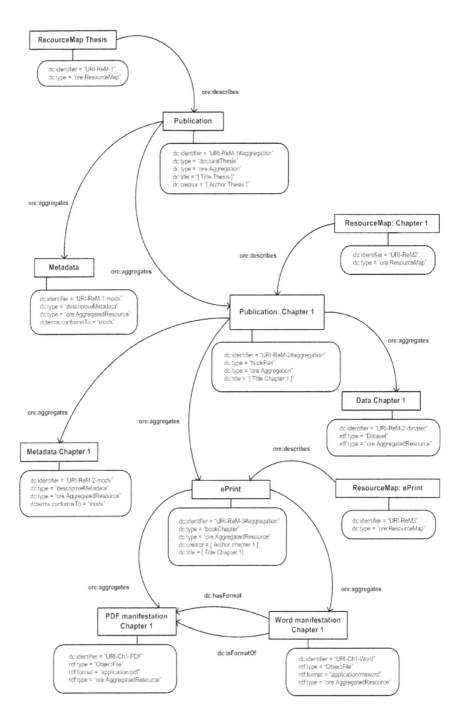

Figure 14. Serialisation of an Enhanced Publication (Example 2)

14. Conclusion

The amount of digitally available research data is growing continuously. Unfortunately, when scientific resources are made available on-line, they are not always published with reliable and consistent metadata. This complicates the retrieval of these research data, which in turn poses a serious threat to an effective reuse of digital resources. A promising approach to improvement of the access to research data is through the enhancement of the traditional publication. This entails that publications are enriched with references to the primary data that were used to produce the insights that are put forward in this text. Scientific publications and research data are currently shared and disseminated through largely the same channels, and publishing these resources in conjunction is now more and more a realistic option. Through Enhanced Publications, researchers can be forwarded effectively to relevant sources, such as underlying data collections, models and algorithms. Such resources can normally not be incorporated fully in the actual publication, but the presence of pointers to the primary data, which are stored separately, should contribute greatly to an improved accessibility of this information. In a sense, the scientific publication will function as metadata for the research data.

Improved visibility of relevant research data benefits the efficiency of scientific processes. Through the use of Enhanced Publications, scientists can leverage current scientific results to generate future discoveries more speedily and more efficiently. Enhanced Publications can also improve the quality of peer review methods, since access to the primary sources enable peers to replicate experiments and to verify the claims that are made in the publication. Importantly, enhancing the traditional publication must improve the visibility and, consequently, the impact of academic studies. With its emphasis on object reuse, the combination of distributed resources and a focus on the lineage of research data, Enhanced Publications must help repository managers to accommodate the demands of academic communication in the 21st century.

References

Berlin Declaration on Open Access to Knowledge in the Sciences and Humanities (Oct. 2003). Accessed April 2008.
http://www.zim.mpg.de/openaccess-berlin/berlindeclaration.html

Borgman, Christine (2007). *Scholarship in the Digital Age: Information, Infrastructure, and the Internet*. Michigan. MIT Press. 2007
Budapest Open Access Initiative (2001-2004). Accessed April 2008.
http://www.soros.org/openaccess/

Candela, Leonardo et al. (2008). *Typed Compound Objects Models for Digital Library Repository Systems*. ISTI Technical Report 2008-TR-023.

Cheung, Kwok et al., "SCOPE – A Scientific Compound Object Publishing and Editing System". T*he International Journal of Digital Curation*, 2 (3), pp. 1-12.

Fink, J. L., & Bourne, P. E. (2007). "Reinventing Scholarly Communication for the Electronic Age". *CTWatch Quarterly, 3* (3), pp. 26-31
http://www.ctwatch.org/quarterly/articles/2007/08/reinventing-scholarly-communication-for-the-electronic-age/

Foulonneau, Muriel and Francis André (2008). *Investigative Study of Standards for Digital Repositories and Related Services*, Amsterdam: Amsterdam University Press.

Hey, Tony and Anne Trefethen (2003). "The Data Deluge: An e-Science Perspective". In *Grid Computing - Making the Global Infrastructure a Reality* (pp. 809-824). Wiley and Sons.

Hunter, Jane (2006). "Scientific Publication Packages. A Selective Approach to the Communication and Archival of Scientific Output". *The International Journal of Digital Curation*, 1 (1), pp. 33-52.

Jeremy, J.C., et al. (2005), "Named graphs, provenance and trust". In *Proceedings of the 14th international conference on World Wide Web*. ACM Press: Chiba, Japan.

Kahn, Robert and Robert Wilensky (2006). "A framework for distributed digital object services". *International Journal on Digital Libraries*, 6 (2), pp. 115-123.

Kircsz Joost G. (1998), "Modularity: the next Form of Scientific Information Presentation?", *Journal of Documentation*, 54 (2), pp. 210-235. http://dx.doi.org/10.1108/EUM0000000007185

Lagoze, Carl and Jane Hunter (2001), "The ABC Ontology and Model", *Journal of Digital Information*, 2 (2), pp. 160-176.

Lagoze, Carl and Herbert van de Sompel, "Compound Information Objects: The OAI-ORE Perspective". May 28, 2007. Accessed July 2008. http://www.openarchives.org/ore/documents/CompoundObjects-200705.html

Lorie, Raymond A. (2001), "Long Term Preservation of Digital Information". In *Proceedings of the 1st ACM/IEEE-CS Joint Conference on Digital Libraries* (JCDL '01), pp. 346-352.

Lynch, Clifford A. (2003), "Institutional Repositories: Essential Infrastructure for Scholarship in the Digital Age". *ARL Bimonthly Report*, Vol. 226.

Murray-Rust, P. and H.S. Rzepa (2004), "The Next Big Thing: From Hypermedia to Datuments". *Journal of Digital Information*, 5 (1).

ORE User Guide – Primer. 11 July 2008 . Accessed July 2008. http://www.openarchives.org/ore/0.9/primer

ORE Specification - Abstract Data Model. 2 June 2008. Accessed July 2008. http://www.openarchives.org/ore/0.9/datamodel

ORE Specification – Vocabulary. 2 June 2008. Accessed July 2008. http://www.openarchives.org/ore/0.9/vocabulary

ORE Specification - Representing Resource Maps Using the Atom Syndication Format. 2 June 2008. Accessed July 2008. http://www.openarchives.org/ore/0.9/atom

ORE User Guide - Resource Map Implementation in RDF/XML. 2 June 2008. http://www.openarchives.org/ore/0.9/rdfxml

Rumsey, Sally and Frances Shipsey (2006). "Scoping Study on Repository Version Identification (RIVER), Final Report". London: Rightscom Ltd.

Seringhaus, M. R. and Gerstein, M.B. (2007). "Publishing Perishing? Towards tomorrow's information architecture". *BMC Bioinformatics*, 8 (17).

Sure, York et al. (2005), "The SWRC Ontology – Semantic Web for Research Communities", In: Carlos Bento et al. [eds.], *Proceedings of the 12th Portuguese Conference on Artificial Intelligence - Progress in Artificial Intelligence* (pp. 218 – 231). Covilha: Springer.

Van de Sompel, Herbert et al. (2004), "Resource Harvesting within the OAI-PMH Framework", *D-Lib Magazine*, 10 (12). http://www.dlib.org/dlib/december04/vandesompel/ 12vandesompel.html

Van de Sompel, Herbert et al. (2004). "Rethink Scholarly Communication: Building the Systems that Scholars Deserve", *D-Lib Magazine*, 10 (9). http://www.dlib.org/dlib/september04/vandesompel/ 09vandesompel.html

Van der Poel, K. G. (2007). *Verkenning van de interesse van wetenschappelijke onderzoekers in WP1-Verrijkte Publicaties en WP2-Collaboratories*. Utrecht: SURFfoundation. http://www.surffoundation.nl/download/20070524_Rapport_Verkenning WP12_vdPoel_def.pdf

Van Horik, R. (2008). "Data Curation". In K. Weenink, L. Waaijers & K. van Godtsenhoven (eds.), *A DRIVER's Guide to European Repositories* (pp. 137-138). Amsterdam: Amsterdam University Press.

Willinsky, John (2005). *The Access Principle*. Michigan. MIT.

PART 3. Sample Datasets and Demonstrator

Arjan Hogenaar, Maarten Hoogerwerf

15. Sample Datasets of Enhanced Publications

15.1 Background

On the Internet one can find much information on related concepts as Compound Objects, Complex Objects and Enhanced Publications. The concepts 'Compound Object' and 'Complex Object' are practically synonymous and are wider than the concept 'Enhanced Publication'. In other words, an Enhanced Publication is a specific type of a Compound Object.

The integration of traditional publications and additional materials will change scholarly work dramatically (Bourne, 2005)[68]. This integration will facilitate access to additional material starting from a traditional publication, e.g. on what data the publication is built, and the other way around, e.g. what publications are written based on a certain dataset.
EP takes optimal advantage of the present digital era. The publication has its origin in the Internet era and datasets, images, software or annotations are associated with it.

EPs are new. As a consequence there was no suitable way to describe them properly yet. Researchers are not aware of all the potential functionalities of EPs. Therefore, we have focused on the selection of suitable material (EPs) and on the formulation of criteria to be met by this material.

Based on data from the literature use cases and user requirements for the demonstrator and the Enhanced Publications can be defined.

15.2 Publication Models

A publication model describes which components are contained in an EP and how they are combined. These components can be specific parts of traditional publications as abstract and hypotheses, but also resources

---

[68] Bourne, P. Will a biological database be different form a biological journal? *PLoS Computational Biology*, (2005), *1* (3), 179-181.
http://dx.doi.org/10.1371/journal.pcbi.0010034

that are normally not part of a traditional publication, like datasets, images, movies, comments, and research descriptions. Not all of these components are necessarily part of an EP. It is up to the creator to define its resources.

In relation to this, the emergence of the EP will lead to new publication models. Two major models can be distinguished:

1. The modular publication model (Joost Kircz) [69]. In this model there is no leading component in the EP. There is a series of ordered objects (and descriptions) that form the EP.
2. The semantic publication model (the Scientific Publication Package, Jane Hunter). It has some resemblance with the modular publication model, but the semantic model has a focus on workflow technologies and on ontologies.

These models have major similarities. They predict the end of the traditional publication model. This traditional model is a static overview of the results of a study. Machines can hardly interpret its structure. In these new models the focus is on the structure of the research/publication, which makes interpretation for both researchers and machines easier.

In the publication models, general complex objects, in which no strict 'central' publication may be observed, can be described as well, but this is beyond the scope of our present work. We define an Enhanced Publication as 'a combined package of a textual resource and additional materials such as original data'.

For now, we assume an Enhanced Publication has at least one textual resource and we will use the following definition:

> "*An Enhanced Publication is a publication that is enhanced with research data, extra material, post publication data, or database records, e.g. the Protein Data Bank. It has an object-based structure with explicit links between the objects. In this definition an object can be an article, a dataset, an image, a movie, a module or a link to information in a database, or it an be part of these*".

---

[69] Kircz, J.G. Modularity: The next form of scientific information presentation? *Journal of Documentation,* (1998), *54* (2), 210-235.
http://dx.doi.org/10.1108/EUM0000000007185

We shall explore the opportunities of combining existing resources, one of which will be a publication.

Interesting developments took place in the Open Archive Initiative (OAI). Because there was a growing need for the exchange and reuse of objects available in the Internet, new standards have been developed. These standards are described via OAI-Object Reuse and Exchange, see OAI-ORE; http://www.openarchives.org/ore/1.0/primer.

OAI-ORE defines standards for the description and exchange of aggregations of Web resources. These aggregations can be perfectly used to describe how EPs are composed and how to exchange them among organisations. A further advantage of OAI-ORE is the fact that via serialisation in ATOM or RDF the descriptions of the EPs can be harvested via the OAI-PMH protocol. Unfortunately, the final description of OAI-ORE (version 1.0) was published too late to incorporate. So, we've worked with its pre-final version (version 0.9).

The new publication models bring many benefits to the scholarly communication process. The dynamic character of EPs may lead to new problems to be solved in the near future. Data can be updated, resources can be added or may disappear, comments may be added or changed and the EPs have boundaries that are not always clear.

This report will focus on static EPs and tries to illustrate the problems to facilitate the discussion between researchers and repository managers about possible needs and solutions.

15.3   Disciplines

At the start of the project we have had discussions on possible differences in EPs in the different disciplines. To keep things simple, we have described the characteristics of the three major research areas: the humanities, the physical sciences and the social sciences. Of course these three disciplines differ in their research approaches, although these differences become less prominent due to the emergence of multidisciplinary, interdisciplinary and trans-disciplinary research.

Humanities mostly study existing raw materials like old/existing texts and artefacts, whereas the natural and technical disciplines concentrate on the experiment and the data that are resulting from these experiments (see Table 1). These are the two extreme forms. The research within the social sciences is very diverse, with on the one hand a 'humanities-like' approach and on the other hand an approach quite similar to the tradition in natural sciences, as can be seen in the neuropsychology field. The most frequent approach in this broad discipline is the one based on questionnaires, which delivers datasets in a rather fixed form.

Discipline	Research area	Typical data
Alpha	Humanities	Text corpora
Beta	Physics, Chemistry, Construction, Life Sciences	Measurements: very specific formats Modelling: CAD,
Gamma	Social Sciences	Statistical data: SPSS, STAT

Table 1. Overview of disciplines

The question remains if the differences between the disciplines may lead to the production of EPs that have distinguishing features to such an extent that these will justify the building of demonstrators for each of these disciplines. After ample discussion and after having studied the OAI-ORE model we reached the conclusion that the abstraction level of this model is sufficient to fit for all disciplines. Differences will exist in the type of additional resources that are used in the disciplines.

An EP-demonstrator based on OAI-ORE will be sufficiently generic to support all kinds of different types of additional resources, including statistical data, measurements and text corpora.

15.4 User Requirements

Building a demonstrator of EPs will only be useful if it meets the users' requirements. A crucial step in the project was gathering information of users to get an idea of what they would expect from such a demonstrator. Together with the DRIVER community and in particular with the Dutch DRIVER participants, united in the Joint Research Unit (JRU), we managed to produce an overview of the most important user requirements. After completion of this inventory we could conclude that the user requirements apply to all disciplines. This was an extra argument to build only one Demonstrator.

We know that both developers and researchers have little experience with EPs. So, it is clear the list as shown below does not mention all possible requirements. For practical reasons, we have divided the requirements into two categories: obligatory ('must have') require-ments and desirable ('nice to have') requirements. More input from researchers is needed to make the Demonstrator more complete.

Name	Description
Cover disciplines	The demonstrator covers all different scientific disciplines: Alfa, Gamma and Beta. There is special attention to the typical kind of data that is used by each discipline.
Use ORE	The demonstrator uses an OAI-ORE description to generate a user-friendly view of the Enhanced Publication.
Display additional material	The researcher can choose what to do with the additional material, depending on the available functionality: download, browse, view, preview.
Navigating between objects	An EP consists of different components and each component can be part of multiple EPs. This creates a network of objects that a researcher can browse.
Identification	The researcher can cite all major components of an EP via a persistent identifier that is displayed with each component.
Relation	The relation of an EP or one of its components with other EP's or components (web resources) has to be visible.

Table 2. 'Must have' user requirements

As expected, the list of 'nice to have' requirements is much longer and is extensible.

Name	Description
Linking parts of the publication	Some terms in a publication refer to items of an ontology, classification system or dataset. The researcher is able to reach the information or data by clicking on that term.
Splitting different parts	A publication can consist of multiple parts such as chapters. Each chapter can have different metadata. The researcher can view each part separately and all parts together.

Name	Description
Combining different parts	All separate chapters can be viewed or printed as one publication.
Versioning the data	It is allowed to update scientific data that has been published. Versioning is needed to adjust any incorrect data.
Updating component alerts	Alert about updates or newer versions of one or more components of the EP.
Normalizing data types	If resources are of the same type, e.g. 'image collection', they can be displayed in the same way. This allows the creation of specific services for specific component-types.
Authentication	Users should be able to authenticate in order to get access to specific resources Some repositories allow open access but want to know who accesses their data.
Annotation	The researcher can add annotations to specific parts of the EP.
Re-use	Every single component of the EP may be re-used in other EP's or traditional publications.
Feedback	The EP must allow feedback from other users. This might be comments, peer reviews, or feedback about the quality of the data.
Harvestability	Service providers can harvest all separate parts of the EP as well as the complete EP.
Overview	Display an overview of all components of the EP as well of all its individual elements of an EP: Article Abstract, Metadata, Related material.
Generate view	Generate e.g. PDF including hyperlinks, comments.

Table 3. 'Nice to have' requirements

15.5 Selection of Datasets of Enhanced Publications

Selecting suitable datasets of Enhanced Publications was not an easy job. First of all we decided to hold on to the principle that a textual resource must be part of the compound object, otherwise this compound object would not be an EP. Further, the concept 'EP' is quite new. Therefore, not every research institution produces EPs already. Luckily, the DRIVER community is very broad. Thanks to our colleagues in Europe we came to an inventory of promising EPs. This inventory has been used in building the Demonstrator.

For building the Demonstrator it is not needed to incorporate all suitable EPs. We need examples of the three different main disciplines and we need examples that will meet the user requirements to show the added value of the Demonstrator. Therefore, the final selection has not been based on a value basis of the EPs available, but just on practical reasons.

Clearly the number of suitable EPs was not the limiting factor in building the Demonstrator. There is a broad variation in disciplines. But how to decide what EPs will be used in the development of the Demonstrator?

Name	Org	Discipline	Description (+ website)
CORF OA+	TUE	Educational Science	CORF/OA+ is a database containing publications, instruments, e.g. online questionnaires, and datasets. http://www.corfstart.nl
E-Crystals	UKOLN	Physics	Database with crystal information. Currently only links to overviews of crystals are available. http://ecrystals.chem.soton.ac.uk
Physics of Fluids	3TU	Physics	Publications combined with video of e.g. falling shampoo. Publications contain links to specific fragments. http://link.aip.org/link/?PHFLE6/19/091106/1
Flame	3TU	Physics	Publications combined with measurements of flames. http://www.ercoftac.nl/workshop11/case11.4/case11.4.html
EDNA	DANS & Leiden	Archaeology	EP with excavation data, including images of the site and of found objects. http://edna.itor.org
Samen in	EUR &	Sociology and	Examples of EPs from several

Name	Org	Discipline	Description (+ website)
Delen	UVT	Economics	disciplines. http://drcwww.uvt.nl/~place/SamenInDelen/
European Value Studies	UvT	Sociology	Longitudinal survey research program on basic human values. http://www.europeanvalues.nl/
E-Theses	UvA	Multidiscipli-nary	Traditional E-thesis, with an accent on the interrelations between chapters of the dissertation. http://dare.uva.nl/dissertations/
IMISCOE	UvA	Demography	A Network of Excellence in the field of Migration Studies. http://www.imiscoe.org/
CAAS	Leiden & TUD	Arts, Chemistry	Analysis of works of art using chemical processes. http://www.caasonline.nl/staging/
Monist	Univ. Bielefeld	(Educational) Neurosciences	Complex neuroscience material. http://www.monist.de/
Hebrew	VU	Linguistics	Queries on Hebrew texts used as research material. http://wivu.dans.knaw.nl/

Table 4. Enhanced Publications suitable for the Demonstrator

16. Demonstrator

16.1 Introduction

It is a rather big step from the theoretical work, selecting datasets of Enhanced Publications, to the more practical work: building a demonstrator. Important issue is the way to describe EPs with OAI-ORE. Another point is how to represent the EPs to the audience in such a way that it remains clear what the components of the EPs are and which interdependencies exist. Finally, the ORE-OAI model leaves it up to the user what kind of serialisation will be used. As stated before, the Demonstrator will just show one of the possible ways to present EPs.

After making the final selection of EPs to be incorporated into the Demonstrator, we made a first sketch of the Demonstrator, based on the User Requirements, the Use Cases and the literature on Object Models and Functionalities. In an earlier stage it was decided to use ORE 0.9 for describing EPs. All EPs will have at least one textual resource that is related to metadata descriptions, datasets, movies or images.

There will be a direct relationship between the Demonstrator and already existing information resources, with an accent on the Dutch resources NARCIS, DANS (EASY), 3TU Datacentre and the Dutch repositories, formerly united in DARE.

Due to limited time and resources we have chosen to elaborate one solution approach. So, alternative or even better representations are possible. More important is the fact that we have succeeded to describe and publish EPs on the Internet using new features, without losing the interoperability of the OAI-PMH protocol for the processing and transferring of metadata of EPs and their component. The EP and every single component will have its own metadata. Above all, the Demonstrator should improve the discussion on and development of services built on repositories of EPs.

The Demonstrator is only available to the DRIVER-community, making copyright and other legal issues a minor issue. In the future we will be confronted with copyright rules. We have decided to present some of these copyright issues in the demonstrator, more precisely in the metadata of the components of the EPs.

We have chosen to build the Demonstrator based on EPs that were delivered to us by our partners in the project. The partners also helped to create OAI-ORE serialisations in RDF.

16.2   Towards a Design

At the start of the Demonstrator project the definition of EPs and the goals and requirements of the demonstrator were unclear. After discussion with the DRIVER community we took the approach that follows. First of all, it was chosen to use the definition already mentioned in paragraph 15.2, built on the definition given in Chapters 7 and 9. Secondly, a long list of possible requirement was divided into 'must haves' and 'nice to haves'. This is the subdivision as given in Tables 2 and 3. These rather functional requirements were the basis for the design below. Other important factors were the experience of the SURFshare project 'Samen in Delen' that also created a demonstrator for EPs and the wish of project members to create an 'offline' demonstrator: one that can be demonstrated without the availability of an internet connection or (local) web servers. The 'Samen in Delen' project showed how OAI-ORE serialisations could be easily transformed into HTML based web pages.

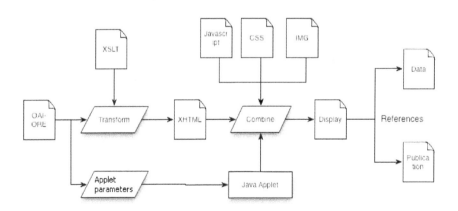

Figure 15. Outlines of design

144

Figure 15 shows the general design of the demonstrator. It shows how OAI-ORE is the basis and how XSLT is used to transform these into XHTML. This XHTML is combined with Java Script, Cascaded Style Sheets (CSS) and images to display the EPs in a user-friendly manner in a web browser. To create a simple overview of the objects contained within an EP a Java Applet would be used to display these graphically. This Applet is integrated into the generated web pages.

The implementation was not without risk because it was not known in advance whether the use of XSLT to transform the OAI-ORE into XHTML would raise any limitations. In this case a server-side translation would be required have more control on the translation. Also a choice had to be made on how to serialise OAI-ORE. None of the reports about OAI-ORE gave a clear decision. Only the makers of SID stated that RDF serialisation is easier to create than ATOM serialisation. The limited amount of time did not allow much research to either the possibilities of client-side XSLT or RDF serialisation.

These uncertainties led to the choice to start with a pilot phase. The EP named 'Flame' was chosen as a model EP. It consists of two cases, each containing a textual description and multiple data files, as shown in Figure 16.

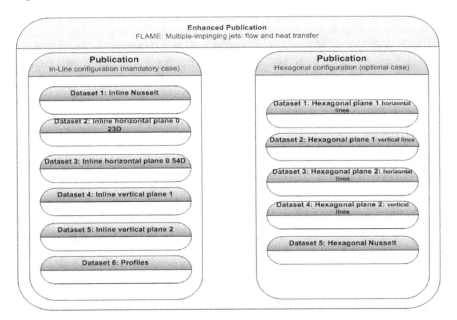

Figure 16. Schematic representation of the EP 'FLAME'

First an HTML mock-up of the EP was created, followed by an RDF serialisation of the EP. The question was now whether we could create a simple XSLT translation between the two of these. If we would not succeed, or if the translation would uncover crucial limitations, then we would stick to creating static HTML representations of EPs.

Thanks to the input from the 'Samen in Delen' project[70] and the work of Magchiel Bijsterbosch a successful translation was created which did not uncover many difficulties for creating a generic transformation for all future EPs. Via an iterative process this generic translation was now formed, other EPs were created, new functionality was added and the layout/usability was improved. In order to create serialisations for the other EPs the help of the organisations that delivered the resources was asked. This uncovered the many possibilities to create EPs from very complex hierarchies to one simple aggregation containing all the resources. Two pre-demonstrations resulted in useful feedback on desired functionality or improved usability. Much was related to the Applet that shows an overview of the objects and their relations. Its functionality was unclear and it had a too prominent position in the EP. These issues were improved for the final demonstrator.

16.3 Final Design

The Final version of the Demonstrator contains six EPs, derived form several sources. All of these resources have been designed without any notice of OAI-ORE and are from different disciplines.

The demonstrator is based on OAI-ORE descriptions that are serialised in RDF, which demonstrates how EPs from different disciplines can be exchanged via e.g. OAI-PMH. It also shows how these EPs can be presented to researchers via commonly available web browsers by transforming the RDF into HTML. The demonstrator shows how users can navigate between the objects of an EP and even between EPs. The related resources, which are identified using persistent identifiers, can be requested or previewed. The demonstrator shows how the relations can also be displayed graphically.

---

[70] Demonstrator SameninDelen: available via:
http://drcwww.uvt.nl/~place/SamenInDelen/ (in Dutch!).

16.3.1 Explanation of the Enhanced Publications incorporated in the Demonstrator

As already mentioned, we had to make a choice of EPs in the construction of the Demonstrator. This choice has been made on the availability of unique features in every single EP. Eventually, the following six EPs have been selected.

FLAME

FLAME is an example of an EP describing two other EPs. On the top level FLAME has a general description, a description of a doctoral thesis and a description of three resources: the human start page and two EPs. These two EPs contain both a description and a number of datasets. It is a typical example for the physical sciences. FLAME is a project of 3TU Datacentre / Delft University of Technology.

HEBREW

HEBREW is a typical example for the humanities. A publication is based on the study of a subset of a huge database, in this case the entire Tenach. The subset is created via queries on the database. On the top level of the EP one can find the general description, the article and the resources, here the queries. These resources themselves are also EPs, giving a general description, the actual query definition, a snapshot of the query result and a live query to the database, the Tenach. HEBREW is a project of the Vrije Universiteit Amsterdam in close collaboration with DANS.

JOURNALISTS

JOURNALISTS is an example of an EP typical for the social science. This example will be elaborated later on, with some illustrations. JOURNALISTS is a project of the Universiteit van Amsterdam and DANS.

SNAPPING SHRIMP RESEARCH (Physics of Fluids)

SNAPPING SHRIMP RESEARCH is another example from the physical sciences. Most peculiar phenomenon is the fact that the EP is covering different publications, where every publication itself is composed of one or more traditional publications with related video material. This example clearly illustrates the additional value of the EP concept. It has become very easy for a user to see all relationships between different objects. It is a project of the Twente University.

YOUTH

YOUTH1 and YOUTH2 are examples of different EPs, sharing one data-set. In other words one single dataset has been used to produce two separate publications. This relation is shown in the description of the dataset as an aggregated resource. YOUTH is an example taken from the social sciences.

IMISCOE

IMISCOE is a very complex EP. IMSICOE stands for International Migration, Integration & Social Cohesion. The IMSCOE publication is a combination of chapters, sometimes with and sometimes without additional information (datasets). The big advantage of the presentation of IMISCOE in the Demonstrator is the fact that the user is immediately able to see what additional information has been provided per chapter. IMSICOE is also an example within the social sciences. IMISCOE is a Network of Excellence uniting 23 European research institutes.

16.3.2. Example of an EP in the Demonstrator

Some screenshots taken from the Demonstrator will help to explain the functionality of the Demonstrator. The EP on 'Journalism' has been used as an example. This example (Figure 17) shows the representation of the EP when a user accesses this very EP. It consists of a dissertation with survey data as additional material. The top of the figure give the general description of the EP, below its components, the textual resources and datasets.

Figure 17. Overview presentation of the EP "Journalists in the Netherlands"

The textual resources originate from the repository of the University of Amsterdam, the resource 'surveydata' from EASY. EASY (the Electronic Archiving SYstem) of DANS gives access to datasets in the humanities and social sciences.

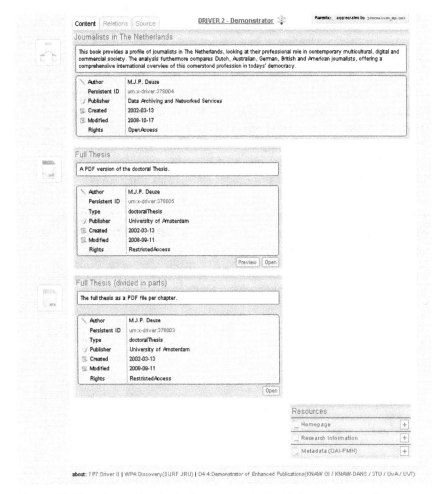

Figure 18. Overview of the textual resources in the EP 'Journalists in the Netherlands'

EPs tend to be very complex. In order to keep the arrangement conveniently, it was decided to work with tabs. The first tab 'Content' shows the general overview of the EP, the three other ones are named 'Relations', 'Comments' and 'Source'. The textual resources of this EP are rather complicated. Figure 18 is the result of the opening of the component 'Journalists in the Netherlands' in Figure 17.

The dissertation is presented as one big file with the total text but also as a collection of separate articles. Here you see the power of the EP: without any problem both forms can be offered to the users. In the right top corner is shown that the presentation in Figure 18 has the general EP presentation as its parent. Every EP and all components have their own Persistent Identifier. EPs offer the possibility to reuse information that is already available in other databases. Is this example you see 'Research Information' as a resource. This resource is a description of the author (Deuze) in NARCIS. NARCIS (National Academic Research and Collaborations Information System) is a portal giving access to Dutch current research, research publications and datasets. NARCIS is a product of the Royal Netherlands Academy of Arts and Sciences (KNAW)[71]. So, in total the EP 'Journalists' is composed of resources originating from the University of Amsterdam, from DANS-EASY and from the portal NARCIS of the KNAW.

As one can imagine, it is sometimes hard to keep an overview of all these components of an EP. In these situations, the user has the possibility to switch to the 'Relations' tab.

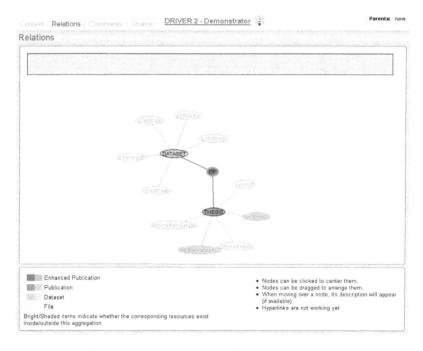

Figure 19. Graphical representation of the EP and its components

---

[71] http://www.narcis.nl

The Relations-tab (see Figure 19) shows the EP in the centre of the graph, with links to the main components, the textual thesis and the dataset. The components or aggregated resources have their own components. The representation of the components in the graph is related to the position of the user in the EP. In this example, the representation is given for the situation related to start view of the EP. Therefore, the EP has a central position. The graphical representation is directly related to the level of the EP that is being viewed. So, if you are viewing a specific dataset, this dataset will be centralised in the representation.

For people interested in the OAI-ORE serialisation in RDF, the Tab 'Source' gives the XML.

Figure 20. RDF Serialisation of the OAI-ORE description of the EP 'Journalists' (partly shown)

For the details and explanation of this RDF-serialisation, we refer to Object Models and Functionalities. Finally, in an environment in which not only the research results but also the raw data is being shared, there is a need for discussion and comment.

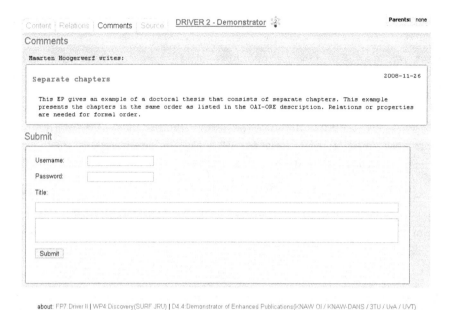

Figure 21. Comments tab of the EP 'Journalists'

Figure 21 shows that readers of the EP can comment on it. For safety reasons, only registered users will be able to comment. This is necessary to prevent the uploading of useless or 'funny' comments.

17. General Discussion and Conclusions

A demonstrator is built that fulfils most of the requirements: EPs from different disciplines have been identified using persistent identifiers and described using OAI-ORE. These descriptions are transformed into web pages that allow navigation between and visualisation of all the described resources. A Java Applet on these web pages is used to visualise the relations between all the resources. Next to these 'must have' requirements there have been many 'nice to have' requirements implemented too, such as the splitting of different parts, the annotations and the reuse of components within an EP. The resulting demonstrator and the choices that have been made resulted in many topics that require discussion. The most important ones are described beneath.

17.1 Choices and requirements

17.1.1 EP creation Tools

In an ideal situation the researchers themselves create the EPs, because they know all about the material used. Building the demonstrator showed that even for ICT professionals it is hard to serialise EPs. User-friendly tools are needed to compose EPs. An example of an OAI-ORE serialisation tool is SCOPE[72].

17.1.2 Serialisation using RDF or ATOM

As yet, there is no definite answer whether to serialise OAI-ORE using ATOM or RDF. For practical reasons the demonstrator uses RDF serialisation. The reason for this is that RDF is more readable and less complex than ATOM. ATOM on the other hand is more common on the web infrastructure. Real life applications are likely to use databases to store relations and will generate the serialisations. It is recommended to have such applications generate ATOM. An advantage of ATOM is that it can easily be transformed into RDF.

---

[72] SCOPE, *A Scientific Compound Object Publishing and Editing System"* [See: K. Cheung, J. Hunter, A. Lashtabeg, J. Drennan,, 3rd International Digital Curation Conference, Washington DC, Dec 11-13, 2007.
http://www.itee.uq.edu.au/~eresearch/papers/2007/IDCC07.pdf]

17.2.3 Abstraction

OAI-ORE leaves much room for implementation. Agreements about obligatory metadata and specific constructs, such as versioning, multiple formats, and sequence-relations are necessary to allow building of services for EPs and proper exchange. The demonstrator uses separate aggregations for such constructs, which were displayed as separate web pages. This endangers the overview of the EPs. Researchers might just want to see a publication with links to related material, not a complex hierarchy of versions and formats. Services that translate complex structures into simplified overviews should be built and too much abstraction avoided.

Because of the late publication of version 1.0 of OAI-ORE, we had to use version 0.9. A comparison taught us that a switchover to OAI-ORE 1.0 will have minor effects on the RDF-serialisation, but will lead to considerable adaptations in the ATOM-serialisation.

Flame demonstrates this case. The EP shows a hierarchy of multiple layers, while the aggregated original website in HTML[73] demonstrates a simple but very effective overview of the two cases, their descriptions and their data files. On the other hand, it should be noted that the website contains no metadata.

17.2.4 Definition of Enhanced Publications

There is much discussion on the definition of Eps. In a generic way it is just an aggregation of (scientific) objects. One trend is to say that an EP should contain at least a textual publication. In particular in the library field this is a popular view. In a more strict way this publication should also be the central part of the publication. However, within the field of the data archives, there is much support to regard datasets also as publications.

Among scholars there is a trend to follow a wider definition of an EP. In this view, e.g. a combination of a video and a dataset may be regarded as an EP. Although the current definition for an EP is clear within this project, there should be awareness that not everyone agrees on the definition and it will be hard to agree on any definition.

---

[73] Test case 11.4: Multiple-impinging jets: flow and heat transfer. Available at: http://www.ercoftac.nl/workshop11/case11.4/

17.2.5 Limitations on Additional Material

The current web architecture allows referral to all possible web resources. Researchers probably want to be able to reference all of these from within EPs. The question raises how much freedom can be offered to the researcher and how much quality and durability needs to be ensured. Possibly there are solutions that satisfy both, but more likely a compromise will be needed. The problems with some resources are:

- A persistent identifier is not always available. In this case, change of location of these resources may make them irretrievable. Therefore, the EP will not be complete anymore and the integrity of its conclusions might decrease.
- The dynamics of resources are often problematic when a component of the EP is a reference to a database. An example is found in the Hebrew EP of the demonstrator. It has referenced to a certain query on a live database. Once changes are made to the database, the result of the query is likely to change. Other researchers are then no longer able to verify the results of the author. Databases that want to provide services for referral need to implement features to execute queries on a specific state of the database. If a database is not static but changes over time, the result of a query on that database should also be added as a dataset to the EP in order to enable future verification.
- A combination of the previous two is the availability of persistent identifiers in databases. High granular referencing requires many persistent identifiers for a specific database. Maintenance and resolution of persistent identifiers becomes more difficult which in turn decreases the persistence of the identifiers as the chance of a correct listing of all persistent identifiers in the EP decreases.
- The web is very anonymous. It is not always known what the origin, the author or the integrity of a resource is.
- Different components of an EP may have different access types. Different resources may originate from different journals or datasets with different access rights. Especially outside the campus of the university of the author, there will be a high risk that parts of the EP will become inaccessible. Within a community such as DRIVER single sign on mechanisms and open access agreements can avoid such difficulties.

17.2.6 Long-term Preservation

The different types of resources and different owners make long-term preservation difficult. Different archives are needed to ensure the durability of the different types and the different owners need to be contacted for archival agreements. In most cases archiving will be on an international scale: the textual resource for example is archived in the Netherlands, whereas the dataset is preserved in Britain.

17.2.7 Versioning

Due to an increasing number of independent resources in an EP, the chance of a change in one of these resources increases also. There needs to be agreement on how to manage these within an EP. Decisions have to be made on whether the version of an EP should change with every single change in version in one of its components and on the rule that an EP should keep referring to the original components.

17.2.8 Conclusions

Although the concept 'Enhanced Publication' (EP) was not well-known among researchers and institutions at the start of this project, it appeared that quite a number of compound publications have already been produced with many characteristics of what we now call an EP. With the help of the DRIVER community we collected cases and defined requirements for the Demonstrator to be built. One of conditions in building a demonstrator of EPs was the reusability and exchangeability of the EPs and of all of its components. Using OAI-ORE, it was possible to realise this functionality. One of the problems that had to be solved was the aspect of the describing of EPs in OAI-ORE. In this project, the team members have translated the existing descriptions into OAI-ORE. Of course this is not the way it should work in the development of real services based on repositories of EPs. Therefore, there is a great need for tools for researchers so that they can compose their own EPs with the right description. In the Demonstrator we have built, the different components of an EP are presented in a clear way, but it is not always obvious what the relations are between these components. So, an extension of the description of the EP is needed. There are several ways to serialise the OAI-ORE. In this project we have chosen the RDF-serialisation, but we are aware of the fact that ATOM or RDF have also their advantages. A broad discussion on this topic should precede the development of services based on EPs. A working Demonstrator is now available, for the moment only to the DRIVER community[74]. It is fully operational only in Firefox 3.0.

---

[74] http://driver2.dans.knaw.nl

PART 4. Long-term Preservation of Enhanced Publications

Paul Doorenbosch, Eugène Dürr, Barbara Sierman,
Jens Ludwig, Birgit Schmidt

18. Introduction

DRIVER II focuses on the aggregation and interoperability of Enhanced Publications (EPs) throughout European digital repositories. Whereas the focus of DRIVER was on purely textual publications, in DRIVER II EPs, which contain many more data formats, will be integrated into the DRIVER infrastructure. This part of the report looks into data models and theoretical frameworks for EPs, and experiences with building an EP demonstrator. Also the long-term preservation aspects of EPs are studied.

For continuity the DRIVER studies, this report uses the definition for EPs as mentioned in Chapter 9.

"Enhanced Publications are envisioned as compound digital objects, which can combine heterogeneous but related web resources. The basis of this compound object is the traditional academic publication. This refers to a textual resource with original work, which is intended for reading by human beings, and which puts forward certain academic claims. Following the Investigative Study of Standards for Digital Repositories and Related Services, a study carried out as part of the DRIVER project, we will use the term 'ePrint'. Foulonneau and André define it as an "electronic version of academic research paper" (p.109). An ePrint is understood as a scholarly work, which contains an interpretation or an analysis of certain primary data, or of derivation from these materials. Examples of ePrints include dissertations, journal articles, working papers, book chapters or reports. [...]"

"Enhancing a publication involves adding one or more resources to this ePrint. These can be the resources that have been produced or consulted during the creation of the text. [...]"

There is a strong relation between this report on long-term preservation aspects and the chapter on *Long-term preservation of Enhanced Publications* in the book 'Emerging Standards for Enhanced Publications and Repository Technology'. Here we will explore some issues, take a closer look at what it means in practice to preserve EPs and give directions for solutions on organisational issues regarding long-term preservation (LTP). EPs may change over time, due to changes in the component part, additions of new resources, instability of data sets, and changing identifiers. Only if an EP is archived together with all of its parts one could speak of a stabilised EP, although this EP is no more than a snapshot, and there is no real guarantee that the original EP is not subject to changes. These questions seem obvious in the case of EPs, but traditional publications or monolithic objects can also be dynamic and can have the same issues. The question arises whether it is useful to preserve an EP. It is an artificial construction of a third party and the elements of an EP are already subjects of archival activities. Also, ORE is chosen as the most effective way for the moment to create EPs, but who knows if this standard is the way of the future?

We will not discuss those questions here, but take the EP in the above definition for granted. We think it is a useful exercise to study the long-term preservation of these EPs. Web resources will have all kinds of links, and we could find out a lot about how we should handle these compound objects by researching the long-term preservation of EPs.

In order to preserve EPs for future use, long-term preservation archives will have to adapt to new standards like ORE and should collaborate more than they currently do. ePrints and research data are treated separately in the current situation, but in the case of EPs the relation between ePrint and accompanying research data must also be preserved. For the Dutch situation, described as a case study here, the challenge is organisational more than technical. Although the situation will differ from country to country, organisational issues will be the same. We do not have the intention of solving all problems identified. Both LTP and EP are rather new phenomena and problems and solutions will undoubtedly change considerably over time. But we do hope to raise awareness for the LTP issue. We are sure the outlines and directions will help the DRIVER community to deal with LTP questions in a better way than before.

This part consists of three chapters:
- An introduction to the connections between IRs and long-term archiving archives;
- A demonstrator for an LTP connector able to handle EPs;
- An overview of various aspects of an archiving agreement between an IR and a long-term archiving facility.

Paragraph 20.3 and Chapter 21 have the Dutch situation as background, the other parts refer to a more generic situation.

Paul Doorenbosch did the overall editing, wrote the chapter about the Dutch situation regarding IRs and LTP and participated in the design of the demonstrator. Barbara Sierman contributed to most of the chapters and wrote the initial version of the chapter on the archiving agreement. Jens Ludwig and Birgit Schmidt were responsible for the overview of aspects regarding long-term preservation and participated in the discussion about the archiving agreement. Eugène Dürr has designed and built the demonstrator, and realised the animation to show the demonstrator process. Maarten Hoogerwerf contributed to the archiving agreement and chapters about the LTP of research data. All partners were involved in commenting text and participated in the discussions that resulted in the final draft. URL's have been last checked in May 2009.

19. Institutional Repositories and long-term Preservation Archives

19.1　Introduction

Although institutional repositories (IR) and long-term preservation archives (LTP) may seem very similar in structure and technology, they differ considerably in their aims. In general, IRs provide of up-to-date end user services while LTP archives are more future-oriented. For example, because of its mission it may be fully acceptable for a LTP archive to have a slow response time and no 24/7 availability if on the other hand it guarantees that its content will be available in decennia to come. Due to these different aims and corresponding different procedures for archiving, a division of labour between IRs and LTP archives makes sense. But with the division of labour between them, they will also have to interact.

The primary task is ingesting of information from an IR to a LTP archive. 'Ingest' is one of the main functional entities of the reference model for an Open Archival Information System (OAIS)[75]. It interacts with the agent who submits the data, performs a set of operations like quality assurance, and ends when the submitted data are packaged into its final form as an Archival Information Package (AIP) and stored in the LTP archive. From the viewpoint of the interaction between the IR and the LTP archive, not every internal operation is relevant. Moreover, not all necessary interactions are regarded as part of the 'ingest' in the OAIS. For example, definition of the authenticity requirements or the creation of a Submission Information Package (SIP) is not part of the OAIS. Therefore it should be noted that 'ingest' has a broader scope in this report than it has in the OAIS reference model. 'Ingest' in the sense of this report covers all the interactions between an IR and LTP archive that are needed to ensure that the latter can accept the responsibility for a submitted data set. It does not only require technical components, i.e. a LTP connector, which realises the technical transfer between two technical systems to establish a connection between these two facilities. It also requires intensive preparation to agree on the

---

[75] Consultative Committee for Space Data Systems: Reference Model for an Open Archival Information System (OAIS). CCSDS 2002
(http://public.ccsds.org/publications/archive/650x0b1.pdf).

terms and conditions of the submission and of the preservation service. This results in archiving agreements, which can take different forms.

One may be tempted to regard such an effort to establish a connection between an IR and an LTP archive as overdone. But one should realise that ingest is a critical part of the LTP. Ingest decisions and procedures have serious consequences for all future activities and errors in the LTP process and may lead to complete failure. E.g. what are the security requirements for an object? What quality standards have to be applied? Ingest is a cost-intensive process but by giving it proper attention one may avoid more expenses later in the data life cycle. Beagrie et al (2008) report that the UK Data Archive sees 42% of their expenses in this process[76]. This may seem overestimated but the *Digitale Bewaring Project* in the Netherlands shows a similar result. Costs of creating metadata ten years after ingest are approximately 30 times more than to provide them during ingest[77].

19.2   Ingest Tasks relevant for an IR-LTP Connection

The following sections give a brief overview on the ingest tasks relevant for an IR-LTP connection[78]. Generally, tasks dealing with objects, processes and management aspects can be distinguished. The order in which these tasks may be performed is not predefined. It depends highly on the situation, e.g. technical constraints.

---

[76] Beagrie, Neil; Chruszcz, Julia; Lavoie, Brian: Keeping Research Data Safe – A Cost Model and Gidance for UK Universities. JISC 2008.
(http://www.jisc.ac.uk/media/documents/publications/keepingresearchdatasafe0 408.pdf).
[77] Nationaal Archief. Costs of Digital Preservation. The Hague, 2005.
(http://www.digitaleduurzaamheid.nl/bibliotheek/docs/CoDPv1.pdf, see p. 15)
[78] This is based at the German guide of the nestor working group for standards (Reference: NESTOR standards working group. Wege ins Archiv. Leitfaden für die Informationsübernahme in das digitale Langzeitarchiv. URN: urn:nbn:de:0008-2008103009 Göttingen, Koblenz 2008. English translation forthcoming.), which itself is based on PAIMAS (Reference: ISO 20652:2006 - Producer-Archive Interface Methodology Abstract Standard (PAIMAS) - Space Data and Information Transfer Systems).

19.2.1 Objects

Although actors generally have a good concept of information objects, the exact nature of them must be clearly communicated between an IR and an LTP archive and built into the connector and the agreements. This covers also aspects of the necessary metadata and the significant properties of the objects for long-term preservation.

Information that should be archived has to be evaluated both on an intellectual and on a technical level. Usually it is the intellectual entity that has to be preserved and not a specific technical representation of the entity[79]. Not files are of interest but documents, photos or measurement results. As a guideline for further decisions, IR and LTP archives need a clear understanding of the information objects that should be archived.

The same intellectual entity may be technically realised by different formats. The main question is which export formats the IR provides. In which technical form will the intellectual entities be provided? Are the formats acceptable for long-term preservation and archival usage scenarios, and can the LTP archive deal with them? Are some formats preferable or are modifications necessary? If the information object consists of different components, like an EP, it may be possible that different components have to be treated differently. And it is worth mentioning that information objects themselves will under no circumstance be modified but that the LTP archive may need to expand its capabilities, e.g. by providing an emulation environment.

The so-called significant properties are important criteria for evaluation of the different options for formats and modifications. Significant properties are those aspects of the intellectual entity which have to be preserved for a designated community and which have to be defined by the IR and the LTP archive.

---

[79] Although exceptions are possible, e.g. computer scientists may be interested not in the content of an information object but only in the way it has been technically realized.

Classic features of significant properties are[80]:
- Content, e.g. text, image, slides;
- Context, e.g. who, when, why;
- Appearance, e.g. font and size, colour, layout;
- Structure, e.g. embedded files, pagination, headings;
- Behaviour, e.g. hypertext links, updating calculations, active links.

Based on the decision pro and contra some significant properties, future preservation measures will be planned, like format decision, migration, and emulations. It is presumably much easier and cheaper for an archive to preserve only the appearance of a web site instead of all of its behaviour as well. But which properties are to be regarded as significant depends on the mission of the LTP archive and repository and the envisaged usage scenarios. Whatever the decision, it has to be well documented. Moreover, it may be advisable to document the significant properties for each information object separately in its metadata.

Beyond information about significant properties, there are plenty of metadata that may be needed. Similar to the evaluation of the information objects, the necessary metadata have to be analyzed. In general, an IR and an LTP archive will focus on different types of metadata. This means that the main question for the LTP archive is: what has to be known to manage the objects for future reuse in a different context?

The OAIS reference model distinguishes the following:
- Descriptive metadata, to discover and access the objects;
- Representation information, technical and semantic background information to use and interpret the objects;
- Reference information, identifiers;
- Context information, relation of the content to other objects;
- Provenance information, what has happened with the object, what is its history;
- Fixity information, checksums to test the integrity.

---

[80] E.g. Wilson, Andrew: Significant Properties Report. 2007. (http://www.significantproperties.org.uk/documents/wp22_significant_properties.pdf).

Not all of these metadata types are of interest for IRs and some of them will probably be generated automatically by the LTP archive, e.g. technical metadata. Nevertheless, the metadata requirements and the types of metadata to be provided by the IR have to be discussed and documented carefully.

19.2.2 Processes

After the question is answered what will be archived, the question presents itself how this will actually be done. How will the information objects and accompanying information be transferred from the IR to the LTP archive? At least three topics have to be addressed:

- How are the information objects packaged for transfer;
- Which validation steps have to be performed by the LTP archive to verify that the objects have safely arrived;
- And of course, what transport technology will be used.

The transfer packages (SIPs in the OAIS terminology) are a kind of common language for both the IR and the LTP archive. Both rely on different ways to manage the information objects and their components internally. Therefore, the definition of transfer packages is an intermediate 'translation layer' for the information objects. For this kind of purpose a wide variety of packaging formats exists already[81].

---

[81] The better known ones are METS (Metadata Encoding and Transmission Standard, http://www.loc.gov/standards/mets/), OAI-ORE (Open Archives Initiative Object Reuse and Exchange, http://www.openarchives.org/ore/) and MPEG 21 - DIDL (Moving Picture Experts Group 21 - Digital Item Declaration Language. http://www.chiariglione.org/mpeg/standards/mpeg-21/mpeg-21.htm).
Others are XFDU (XML Formatted Data Units, http://sindbad.gsfc.nasa.gov/xfdu/) from the Consultative Committee for Space Data Systems (CCSDS) responsible for the OAIS, BagIt. (http://www.cdlib.org/inside/diglib/bagit/bagitspec.html) which is a minimalistic approach of the California Digital Library, RAMLET (Resource Aggregation Model for Learning, Education and Training, http://www.ieeeltsc.org/working-groups/wg11CMI/ramlet), Content Packaging XML Binding for IMS (Instructional Management Systems). (http://www.imsglobal.org/content/packaging/) or SCORM (Sharable Content Object Reference Model, http://www.adlnet.gov/scorm/). For a detailed discussion in the context of

Regardless of the format chosen, a number of further decisions are crucial for the process. In particular, one has to decide on how information objects are mapped to the transfer packages. A single package does not necessarily contain a complete object, although this is often the simplest choice. Other variants may make sense too. If, for example, very large objects have to be transferred, it may be necessary to split them among different packages. Or if a certain object is required by a lot of other objects, it may be convenient to transfer them all together in a single package.

Beyond the mere distribution of information objects in packages, the IR and the LTP archive have to make sure that the structure of a single information object can be reconstructed. This includes questions like which metadata sets belong to which files, which dependencies on other information objects exist or which object is the start file of a web site?

Until the information object is stored in the LTP archive several processes may produce errors. To ensure that only the correct objects are archived, the transferred objects have to be validated. The exact test types depend on the situation but typically tested properties include the following issues:
- Completeness, are all components and metadata sets present;
- Integrity, is the object unchanged;
- Technical validity, has the object the required quality, e.g. is the file format valid.

Rigid validity tests are probably a good thing, but one has to be sure about the required degree of compliance and the consequences if a test is not passed. If an object does not pass the test, the IR should be notified and a correct version may be submitted again. But what if a valid version of the object is not at the disposal of an IR for some reason? That is, there may occur circumstances under which the object has to be accepted anyhow, such as archiving agreement and preservation levels. The IR and the LTP archive should therefore be very clear about what kinds of tests are performed. Even the tools involved need clarification because different tools may produce different results.

---

81 continued. Enhanced Publications see Woutersen-Windhouwer S., R. Brandsma, Enhanced Publications: State of the Art. In: Vernooy-Gerritsen M. (ed), Enhanced Publications. Linking Publications and Research Data in Digital Repositories. SURF, Amsterdam University Press 2009

The transfer or transport itself involves a number of options. The IR may upload the data into a staging area on a server of the LTP archive, the data could be harvested by the LTP archive, it can be transferred offline. Legal and security requirements may put constraints on the choice of the transfer method, the kind and amount of objects to be transferred and the available technical infrastructure in general. The IR and the LTP archive have to agree on the transfer method and also on the transfer steps and their time frame. This is partially predefined by the chosen transfer method. But open questions remain: when and how often transfers will be executed, what feedback mechanisms are used and how the transfer itself will be tested. In particular, new ways of transfer between an IR and an LTP archive have to be tested thoroughly before they can be used productively.

19.2.3 Agreements and Documentation

Another crucial component of the ingest process is the documentation. All planning and contractual decisions have to be documented, as well as the actual results of the ingest processes. This documentation does not only provide a guideline in implementing the connection and in re-solving issues during the ingest process, but in the long run is the only instrument to audit the connection and the authenticity and integrity of transferred objects. Also, a transparent and citable documentation sup-ports the trustworthiness of the involved institutions. For these reasons it is necessary to preserve not only the ingested objects but also the documentation related to this ingest, e.g. as part of the provenance metadata of the objects or linked to them. The planning process should be documented in detail in an archiving agreement. In general, all tasks mentioned above have to be considered in these agreements.

Another essential component of the documentation is a detailed protocol of the ingest process itself, containing all activities and rules for deviations from the presumed course of events.

This protocol should in particular include the following items:
- A list of the ingested intellectual entities and their files;
- The name of the actors;
- Date and timestamps;
- Performed tests and results;
- Modifications or conversions applied to the objects;
- Error messages.

The definition of legal and financial aspects will be covered by a separate document. In order to achieve a solid connection and trustworthy preservation process, a reliable legal, financial and institutional basis is needed. The most basic issue is the identification of the legal entities and the responsible actors for the IR and the LTP archive and definition of their relationship. Additionally, the costs of the LTP archive may have to be covered and may be stipulated in these documents. And if costs are addressed, possible benefits have to be addressed as well. What are the obligations for the archived objects, and is there a warranty and liability for the archiving process? These questions may look a bit too formal for situations where the IR and the LTP archive are part of the same institution. But certainly some issues have to be solved, even if no legal binding document between IR and LTP archive is necessary. In any case, intellectual property rights and copyright questions in particular will be an issue for the long-term preservation. Already, the most basic kind of preservation fails if the LTP archive is not permitted to create copies of objects. If you are not allowed to make redundant copies you cannot ensure the bit stream preservation of an object. Also, the reuse of ePrints and data sets wouldn't be possible. Therefore it is absolutely inevitable to solve these questions before the ingest starts and to include corresponding clauses in the appropriate documents to gain the authorisation for all actions necessary to preserve the digital object.

19.3 Connection between Repositories and LTP Archive

In this section we take a closer look at the Dutch situation regarding the connection between IRs and the LTP archive, as case study of such a connection. Although parties hosting repositories in the Netherlands are the primary parties to take responsibility for long-term availability of the scientific output of their own community, together with the National Library they have established an effective network in order to guarantee really long-term preservation.

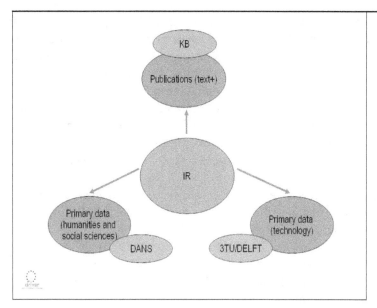

Figure 22. Dutch long-term preservation landscape for research

KB[82] is the National Library of the Netherlands. It takes care of the long-term preservation of publications. Digital Archive and Networking Services (DANS)[83] has taken responsibility for long-term preservation of primary data in the humanities and social sciences, and an alliance of the three Dutch Technical Universities has established a common data centre at the University of Delft (3TU) [84]. There is no known party for the long-term preservation of medical data in the Netherlands. Besides the ones mentioned, there are some smaller institutions that maintain their own LTP instance such as the International Institutions for Social History. Other parties are active in the LTP field, such as the Institute for Sound and Vision (audio and video), the National Archives, and the regional and local archives, but these are not specialised in the results of scientific activities. The Netherlands Coalition for Digital preservation (NCDD) [85] carries out a survey to take stock of the status quo (2009) of digital preservation in the Netherlands.

The data archive at 3TU is still under construction. The data archive at DANS has been in existence already for quite a few years, and was

[82] KB: http://www.kb.nl/index-en.html

[83] DANS: http://www.dans.knaw.nl/en/

[84] 3TU: http://www.3tu.nl/en/

[85] NCDD: http://www.ncdd.nl/en/index.php

renewed five years ago when DANS was established as a new institute dedicated to its archival task and the reuse of existing data in the humanities and social sciences. A very significant difference between the archiving processes of DANS and KB is that KB gathers the publication by harvesting and uses a nearly fully-automated ingest procedure, while researchers have to deposit their data actively at DANS and DANS describes and standardises some parts of the data and meta data manually. The focus of this report is on the process at KB, but we will pay attention to the other two archival instances where relevant.

The Dutch network for access to, and long-term preservation of, research results, has emerged from a project called DARE[86] (Digital Academic Repositories) that ran from 2003 until 2006. In this project the Dutch research universities and a number of research institutions organised local repositories and made agreements about formats and protocols. A unified access point came available via the NOD[87] (Dutch Research Database), an institution of the Royal Netherlands Academy of Arts and Sciences (KNAW). The KB, being the national library, took care of the long-term preservation of the academic publications. The DARE-project was conducted by SURFfoundation[88], the collaborative organisation in which research universities, universities of applied sciences and research institutions aim to innovate education and research by means of ICT. The original DAREnet, nowadays called NARCIS[89], has been expanded over time with other research institutions and with universities for applied sciences.

All Dutch universities and a growing number of scientific institutions and universities of applied sciences in the Netherlands make the scientific output of their institutions available on the net by means of an IR. These IRs are structured according to local policies. There is no common system or format in use for IRs, but there are agreements about how and in what format the metadata and objects can be harvested and what selection of data will be harvested for long-term preservation[90]. Although an IR could hold every kind of object, the selection or set for long-term preservation by the KB contains objects in

---

[86] DARE-project: http://www.kb.nl/hrd/dd/dd_projecten/projecten_dare-en.html; now-a-days available under the acronym: NARCIS.

[87] NOD: http://www.onderzoekinformatie.nl/en/oi/

[88] SURFfoundation: http://www.surffoundation.nl/en/Pages/default.aspx

[89] NARCIS: http://www.narcis.info/?wicket:interface=:1::::

[90] See appendix A.

a limited number of file formats, which are mostly text oriented (ePrints). Objects could be simple objects or compound objects, such as a dissertation with a number of chapters, each as a separate file. Once an object is placed in the LTP system (KB e-Depot)[91], an IR can't withdraw it anymore. The objects ingested in KB e-Depot can be retrieved by the KB-website. The metadata presented also contain a URL to the original place of the publication in an IR. An IR can ask the KB to make a copy of its publications in the LTP archive, and deliver them back. The e-Depot should not be considered as a backup system, but it can be used to rely on in case of emergency.

19.3.1 Objects

Institutional Repository (IR)
The IR is responsible for assigning a record to a specific set and for updating the modification date. IRs make their own policies on whether an object will be part of the set to be harvested for long-term preservation. For KB the only limitations are that access to an object must not be restricted, and that the files must belong to a certain file format and version of that format, according to a limited list. Adding a new file format or format version is the decision of the LTP organisation (KB). The OAI-PMH protocol is used for harvesting. The IR has to install an OAI-server and communicate to the KB the actual base URL for harvesting, the metadata prefix used in the harvesting set and the name of the set(s) to be harvested for long-term preservation.

---

[91] E-Depot: The KB has developed a specific workflow for archiving electronic publications. Elements of this workflow are: accept and pre-process; generate and resolve identifiers; search and retrieve publications; and identify, authenticate and authorize users. The technical heart of the e-Depot system is IBM's DIAS (Digital Information and Archiving System). The DIAS solution provides a flexible and scalable open deposit library solution for storing and retrieving massive amounts of electronic documents and multimedia files. It conforms to the ISO Reference Open Archival Information System (OAIS) standard and supports physical and logical digital preservation. The DIAS solution allows the manual as well as automated ingest of digital information (assets) into the system. Once the asset is successfully stored it will be maintained and preserved. Preservation functionality will be enhanced in future DIAS versions to generate signals when stored assets must be converted or migrated to ensure their availability.

Every object is 'described' by an MPEG21-DIDL[92] file, containing the metadata and the URL to the resource or to the different parts of a compound object. The resources themselves are not included in the container. The sequence of the references to the different parts of an object mirrors the order of these parts in the context of the compound object as a whole. The DIDL-file contains a modification date that is used for the decision whether an object is new or modified since the last harvest and whether it should be harvested again. A modified object will be handled as a new object. The current KB-system (DIAS) is not able to accommodate versioning. The existing object stays in the system and the new object is added as a new object. Both identifiers are merged into one metadata record. For the public only the newest version is retrievable.

Before 2009, the IRs and the KB agreed upon a simplified DIDL-container (DARE-DIDL). Starting January 1st 2009, the use of the standard MPEG21-DIDL (version 2.3) is compulsory[93]. We describe the situation from January 1st 2009. The DIDL container includes biblio-graphic metadata in DC-format. Publications (resources) are not included in the DIDL-container. The container holds URLs to the resources in the repositories, which are in principle persistent[94]. The storage of the resources in the IR could be organised in different ways, as a database or as a file system. This is not relevant for the KB as long as it is accessible via a standard Internet protocol.

---

[92] MPEG21-DIDL (or just DIDL): Digital Item Declaration Language. It specifies a uniform and flexible abstraction and interoperable schema for declaring the structure and makeup of Digital Items. Digital Items are declared using the Digital Item Declaration Language (DIDL) and declaring a Digital Item involves specifying its resources, metadata and their interrelationships: (http://xml.coverpages.org/mpeg21-didl.html)

[93] In January 2008, the latest version of the MPEG21-DIDL specification for use in DARE was completed and accepted: MPEG21-DIDL Document Specifications for repositories, by Maurice Vanderfeesten et al. (https://www.surfgroepen.nl/sites/oai/complexobjects/Shared%20Documents/D IDLdocumentSpecification_EN_v2.3.doc)

[94] Although Dutch libraries are aware of the necessity of using some kind of persistent identifiers and are currently implanting them, there is no guarantee a PI is added to every single object.

174

19.3.2 Processes[95]

Harvesting

The OAI-PMH protocol is used for harvesting. With an agreed interval, a scheduler starts the harvesting process for a repository, starting from the last harvest date for that specific repository. The DIDL-container is transferred to the harvester. The data in the original DIDL-file will not be changed during the process from harvest to ingest, but there are some additions to the file such as information about the owner, administrative metadata, and the file format and its version in a separate part of the process. In a subsequent action the objects themselves are being transferred. Objects and DIDL are packed in a batch file with a unique ID required by the e-Depot based on the DIDL-ID.

These steps are done in an application dedicated to the harvesting of IRs. Next stage in the process is to check the file format and the version number of the file format and add this information in a standardised form and an internal form to the metadata. This characterisation is done by a DROID-implementation (Digital Record Object Identification)[96]. Acceptance or denial of an undesirable file format is done later in the process. Only if DROID does not recognise a file format/version or could not assign a unique format ID to a file, the whole batch is transferred to a special folder. The implementation of the DROID-service assigns a PUID[97] [PRONOM Unique Identifier] to every object file and translate this characterisation to an internal number required by the e-Depot system. The generated PUID is added to the metadata for possible future use. From here on, the batch file is handled in the same way as the mainstream of publications for long-term preservation.

Pre-process

Batch files are transferred to the e-Depot environment. They arrive in the so-called post office. From here the process continues fully automatically until the object is stored in the DIAS-system, the LTP storage. If a critical error appears in one of the performed controls, the whole batch is rejected and placed in a separate environment for

---

[95] We haven't described the complete process, but only the steps relevant for this book.

[96] DROID: http://droid.sourceforge.net/wiki/index.php/Introduction

[97] PUID: PRONOM (Persistent) Unique Identifier:
http://www.nationalarchives.gov.uk/aboutapps/pronom/puid.htm

analysis. Once the problem is solved the batch is replaced in the post office once again and follows the whole process from the beginning. In the post office a virus check takes place. After that, the pre-ingest process checks filenames and some administrative metadata.

The end of the pre-process is the so-called BatchBuilder. Here, file format and file format version, the assigned internal characterisation mark, are checked against a list of acceptable formats/versions and a unique internal identifier is added to the metadata and to the batch, the object as a whole and the metadata. Files and metadata are packed together into SIP and stored in DIAS as AIP. A copy of the metadata is delivered to the general retrieval database of the KB, the catalogue.

As mentioned before, this is the standard procedure for all publications that are stored in the e-Depot. For IR-harvested objects there is only one exception to this process. As bibliographic metadata come from the repositories in DC-format and the BatchBuilder is at this moment only able to handle a proprietary XML-format there is a dedicated style sheet in place to extract the DC information and convert it to this proprietary-format[98].

The products of the pre-ingest procedure are:
- A SIP with the resources and a file with the original metadata (DIDL-container) enriched with some technical and preservation metadata;
- An XML file with the bibliographic metadata.

Storage and retrieval
The SIP file is stored in the LTP system (DIAS) as an AIP. The LTP archive is accessed from the KB catalogue. Some data fields are extracted from the metadata-file to update the authentication database to mark the object as open access and to support the retrieval functionality.

The metadata-file is processed by a style sheet that converts its content to DCX[99]. A standard update mechanism checks if there is already an

---

[98] In figure 23 referred to as EWTIJ-format.

[99] DCX has the possibility to add extended tags to the official Dublin Core, without affecting this core. Applications that can handle DC can simply skip the extended fields. If an application knows about the 'meaning' or functionality of the extended fields (they are published in a metadata-registry) it can use them.

entry for this object in the KB-metadata-database and if so, merge the old and new metadata. The DCX file is stored in the KB-database and indexed. Links in the metadata makes it possible to retrieve the object from the LTP system (DIAS) or directly from the IR where it was harvested from.

19.3.3 Archiving Agreement

In December 2006, the first work agreements between 13 Dutch universities, the Royal Netherlands Academy of Arts and Sciences (KNAW), The Netherlands Organisation for Scientific Research, and the Koninklijke Bibliotheek (KB, National Library of the Netherlands) as the counter party, were signed. This was not a truly archiving agreement and therefore called work agreement.

The 2006-version of this agreement was a first effort to regulate the relationship between IRs and the long-term preservation archive. KB is in the process of revising this agreement. A draft of this document is given as an appendix to Chapter 22. But it is still not an archiving agreement. To maintain the network, the SURFfoundation installed some working groups under its own coordination. The main working group, in which decisions about the network are being prepared, is the assembly of repository managers.

19.4   New Developments

In this section we give a short overview of current development in issues regarding LTP-infrastructure.

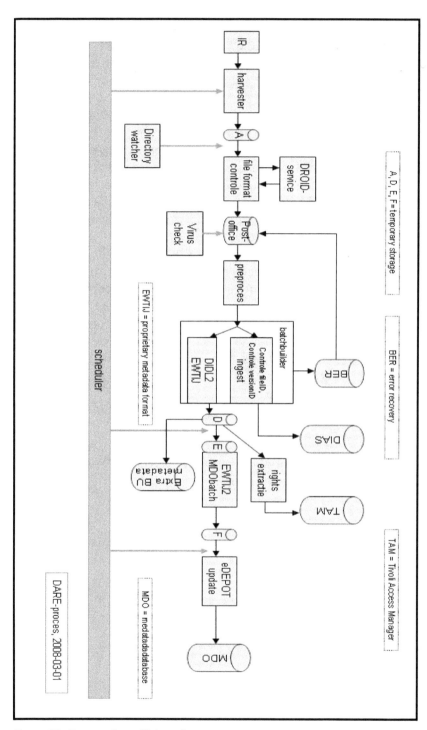

Figure 23. Process from IR to e-Depot

178

File Format Services

Determining the file format and version of the digital object is a prerequisite for the long-term preservation of the object. Several initiatives support LTP archives in this activity, of which the new developments regarding JHOVE[100], GDFR[101] (Global Digital Format Registry) that recently became Unified DFR (UDFR)[102], and AONSII[103] are of interest for DRIVER II.

Persistent Identifiers

Digital objects need a persistent identifier (PI), so that researchers are able to correctly identify the digital source over the years. Although the actual use of persistent identifiers can be improved, there are initiatives to create the necessary infrastructure for PIs.

Archival Concept/ Repository Models

The OAIS Reference model acts as a standard in the digital preservation community. As this is a conceptual model, it needs to be translated into practical implementations. Several projects are initiated to investigate this, especially as deliverable of projects funded by the European Commission (PLANETS[104], SHAMAN[105] and CASPER[106]).

Preservation Strategies

One of the results of the European project PLANETS will be the Preservation Planning tool PLATO, an automated decision tool, based on the PLANETS preservation planning methodology. It assists organisations in defining their requirements, the collection profiles and other essential information for preservation actions. It will evaluate this input and will give a recommendation how to best perform the preservation action for that particular collection. PLATO will also be of advice on the use of certain tools for the action.

Developments in Emulation

Hardware emulation is the preservation action in which the original hardware architecture is mimicked through software. This supports the

---

[100] JHOVE: http://hul.harvard.edu/jhove/

[101] GDFR: http://www.gdfr.info/

[102] UDFR: http://www.gdfr.info/udfr.html

[103] AONSII: http://hdl.handle.net/1885/46645

[104] PLANETS: http://www.planets-project.eu/

[105] SHAMAN: http://shaman-ip.eu/shaman/node/44

[106] CASPAR: http://www.casparpreserves.eu/

process of bringing digital objects back to life in their own environment without changing the object itself, but by changing the environment. The Dioscuri emulator is available[107]. But for the actual rendering of a digital artefact, the emulation tool only will not be enough. Information is needed about dependencies on the original hardware and software environment. Besides that, the original software should be available and there should be a mechanism to match these requirements so that the emulator can work properly. The work done on emulation in Planets is currently extended in a new project: KEEP (Keeping Emulation Environments Portable), with support of the European Commission. The goal of this project is to build an emulation access platform, where several emulators will be available, in order to allow end-users to access digital objects in their own environment. Another area that KEEP will cover is offering means to transfer data from outdated computer media carriers to new (virtual) carriers or storage devices, for example disk images.

19.5   Conclusion

Starting with an overview of the main issues in the long-term archiving of digital publications, we continued by describing the existing connection between the Dutch university IRs and the LTP archive in the KB, as an example. This framework was realised during the DARE-project (2003-2006) one of the original components for the building of the Driver infrastructure. Describing this example is useful because an overall conclusion is that for EPs it is not necessary or efficient to create a whole new infrastructure, but that we should think more in the direction of expanding the existing infrastructure with a facility for the accommodation of the EP-aggregation.

---

[107] Dioscuri: http://dioscuri.sourceforge.net

20. A Demonstrator for an LTP Connector

20.1 Introduction

This chapter describes a process for transferring an EP from a repository to a long-term preservation archive and a demonstrator process of transferring an EP from a Dutch Driver repository to the test environment of the Dutch LTP archive of publications at the KB.

The primary target is to develop a working prototype, a proof of concept, for archiving of EPs inside a LTP archive. We have limited the demonstrator to the e-Depot of the National Library of the Netherlands (KB). The Netherlands is to our knowledge the only country within the Driver community with a regularly operating service for transferring academic digital publications to a LTP archive. For this reason we take the Dutch situation as a reference point for the EP-LTP demonstrator. It should be noted that access is not part of the scope of this demonstrator.

20.2 Objects, Enhanced Publication

An EP differs from a common publication in the sense that an EP is a compound digital object that may consist of various heterogeneous but related web resources. Each of these web resources is an atomic entity in itself and can be used on its own. In this discussion, it can be expected that each part of an EP can be referred to uniquely. The EP consists of the complete set of these atomic entities. The underlying idea is that the whole entity offers more than the sum of its parts. This advantage is something a repository wants to offer to its audience.

What is an EP? The definition of an EP, as formulated in Chapter 9 is the starting point: EPs can be defined as compound digital objects, which combine ePrints with one or more metadata records, one or more data resources, or any combination of these.

Since the DRIVER project focuses on academic publications in the traditional sense, it is assumed here that an enhanced publication must minimally include one ePrint.

This definition supposes that an EP has a digital text publication directed as ePrint to start with, and that all the other object parts are related to it. The same report states that parts of the compound object might be distributed over several repositories, even in different countries. Each part of the EP is an autonomous entity and understandable on its own.

As an EP consists of different parts, the main question is how to store the whole EP into the LTP archive. In other words how to get the various parts in different repositories into one LTP archive or in several ones, as in the Dutch situation, and offer the future user this EP as one complete entity.

20.3 Transferring Enhanced Publications to the e-Depot

20.3.1 Background

The current e-Depot procedure harvests metadata and content for a single item document. The metadata is first encapsulated by an IR into an MPEG21-DIDL container and then transferred to the KB. After parsing the DIDL at the KB, the documents are retrieved and transferred to the e-Depot. The KB initiates the transfer of all items.

To accommodate EPs, we propose to extend this procedure in such a way that also EPs consisting of aggregates of items, described by ORE-graphs[108], and the objects can be handled. As for the DRIVER II project we assumed that the repository manager places an ORE-graph in a special set in an IR. We assume that somewhere and at a certain moment in time an EP comes into existence and 'enters' the repository for the EPs, the IR-EP. How, why and by whom this event shows up, is considered outside the scope of this activity.

An automated procedure for the harvesting of data and storage in an LTP-archive exists only for ePrints. The demonstrator focuses on the procedure for an ePrint within an EP. The procedure for transferring other objects of the EP to other LTP archives is prepared but not operational.

---

[108] The use of ORE is necessary for this demonstrator. The choice for OAI-ORE is discussed in part 3 of this book.

20.3.2 Requirements

On the input side we will have a repository[109] that stores the EPs. The EPs are represented by a number, at least one, of hierarchically ordered resource descriptors in RDF/XML. In these descriptors ORE extensions, mainly the relations *ore:aggregates* and *ore:isAggregatedBy*, represent the dependency between the components of the EP. Each component has its descriptor. The components all have a descriptor and the content is either locally present in the same repository or resides elsewhere on the internet. In both cases, the components are supposed to have a persistent identifier in the form of a URI. In some descriptors only the minimal required metadata will be present. Other metadata in other formats also can be present as a component of the EP. We have taken the definition of Chapter 9 for an EP. A typical EP might look like figure 24 in its graph representation.

The content links can point to components in other repositories via persistent identifiers.

For this demonstrator, we made some assumptions about the structure and implementation of the abstract descriptions and definitions given above.

Firstly, we made a distinction between major and minor resources within an EP. Major components are the ePrint, the (DC) metadata set for the entire publication and a dataset. Major resources have their own persistent identifier. Each of these major components can have minor components, like figures and tables in an ePrint, or several individual files in a dataset. These minor components have no permanent identifier. They are supposed to be bundled together with their major component in e.g. a DIDL like structure or zip file.

---

[109] This can be a very simple file system directory in the demo.

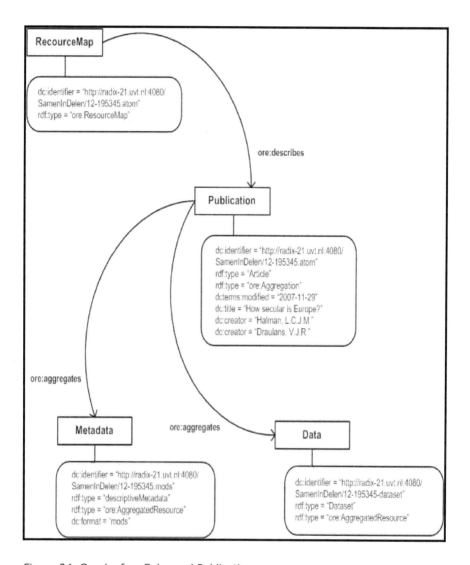

Figure 24. Graph of an Enhanced Publication

We decided to take the following implementation structure for an EP as a working definition:

- One root node file with a list of all components in the EP, written in RDF/XML. This represents the resource map with the links to the major components;
- The Aggregation list with these components and an entry for each aggregated Resource are all include in one <ep_name>.xml file;

184

- Resource descriptions of the following major components are always available: the ePrint, the metadata set of the entire EP, and a dataset. Introduction of the concept of a 'null document/resource or object' handles cases where one or more items are (temporarily) missing;
- For each major component there is also one individual aggregate entry, which provides the links to the content;
- We thus limit the depth of the graph to two levels: the root-node and one level below it.

20.3.3 The LPT Demonstrator

The feasibility proof of the extension from a simple publication structure into a full EP with all its flexibility is the main objective of this demonstrator. After ample discussions, we concluded that this extension could be realised through an analogy of the current procedure for publications as described in Paragraph 19.3. We therefore propose a third entity in the relations between the IR and the LTP archive, an EP-Transformer.

The functionality of this EP-Transformer is to parse the set of resource descriptors of the EP, construct the dependency graph and recursively check whether all references can result in a local copy of all components of the EP. The LTP archive is thus ensured that all resources are retrievable.

There are some reasons for not including the objects themselves into the DIDL-container:
- Retrieving the objects directly from the IRs gives the LTP instance a direct responsibility relation with the IR. Using a third instance makes the relation less trustworthy. The longer the process and the more stages it has, the bigger the risk of unlikely, unforeseen and unregistered changes in the objects;
- The amount of data can be very large, especially if there are video or high-resolution images in the EP. Transferring and storing them more than absolutely necessary is not efficient;
- More practically: not storing the objects in the container prevents interference in the current e-Depot process that is designed for subsequent and separate harvesting of metadata and objects and integrating them only during the ingest procedure. Nevertheless, if an archival instance asks for a container with both metadata and objects, this could be arranged by adapting the EP-transformer to

it. A proof-of-concept of such a mechanism was made in the preparation phase of the LTP demonstrator.

When all components are available, they are incorporated into several containers in MPEG21-DIDL format together with the descriptors; one container for each LTP archive. This format allows for a hierarchy of the components included in the container. A decision mechanism should decide which documents will be stored in which LTP archive[110], due to the division that has been made between the different existing LTP archives in the Netherlands. KB handles only 'traditional' documents. Each DIDL contains a complete and identical representation of the EP. A special case is the preservation of the root component in the ORE descriptor hierarchy. This may be even a null-document, thus a descriptor without content. Such an EP-container is then transferred to the KB. Here it can be treated as a single item for storage. The procedure can be visualised in Figure 25.

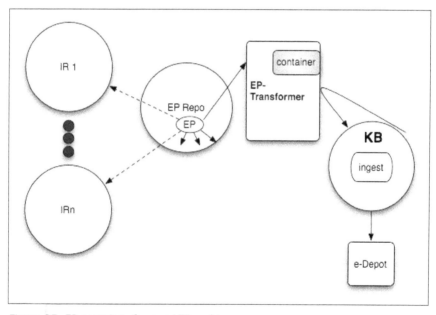

Figure 25. EP container for one LTP archive

The complete-procedure can be visualised by extending this scheme, as in Figure 26.

---

[110] See Paragraph 20.4 for some of the decision issues.

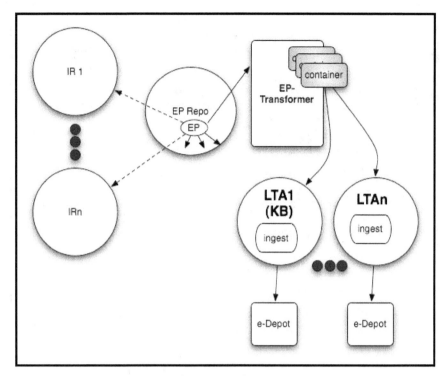

Figure 26. EP containers for several LTP archives

Detailing the steps that have to be taken at the EP-Transformer and the LTP archives may refine the procedure. Again we take the KB as LTP archive example.

The demonstrator process consists of two parts. First we prepared an EP to be harvested by an LTP archive. This part is completed. The software is written by Eugène Dürr (University of Delft)[111]. The second part is the transfer of the ePrint, the part harvested by the KB to the ingest environment of the e-Depot at the KB, after which it follows the route of all other material gathered for LTP[112]. To show the process and decisions made in it we created an animation[113].

---

[111] The software, instructions for usage and the results are available at http://research.kb.nl/DRIVERII/EP-LTP_demonstrator.html..

[112] See Paragraph 19.3.2.

[113] This animation is available at the same site and at de SURFnet video portal, http://www.surfmedia.nl/medialibrary/item.html?id=D5CHvHq2d27nAnHDhOrbx aOo

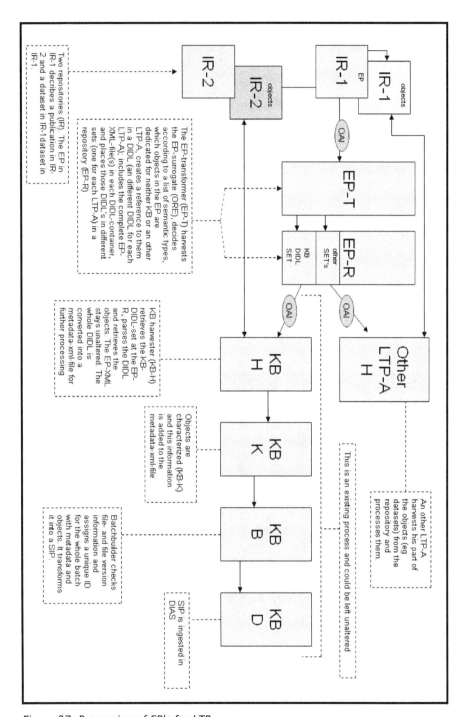

Figure 27. Processing of EP's for LTP

188

Content Type of Publication

A typical EP consists of one or more ePrints and some data sets. In the Dutch situation there are currently three LTP archives:

- KB for publications;
- DANS/KNAW for humanities and social sciences data set;
- 3TU Data Centre for beta and technical data sets (under construction).

In the EP Transformer a decision has to be made where to send which component of the EP for long-term preservation. There are two decisions to make. The first one is to decide which part of the EP is an 'ePrint' and which part is the 'data set'. The second decision is where de different parts should be stored for long-term preservation. Both decisions cannot always be made fully automatically with the current set of meta-data fields in the ORE resource descriptors. To solve this problem we recommend the addition of a special meta-data field in each component of the EP with the name of the target LTP. In this way the responsibility for where parts of the EP will be stored is where it belongs, at the origin of the EP, being the Institutional Repository. Without these extra LTP meta-data items we had to base our decisions on the currently available required fields.

For the first decision, the split between the ePrint and the dataset parts, we can use the value of the attribute 'semanticType' used in the individual ORE resource descriptor(s) and also in the root document node of the EP. If a component has the semantic type: info:eu-repro/semantics/publicationType or purl.org/eprint/type, it should be an ePrint and can be sent to the long-term archive for ePrints. In the Dutch situation, this is the National Library of The Netherlands, the KB. If the resource descriptor gives as semantic type: 'Dataset' (http://purl.org/dc/dcmi/Dataset) it should be a data set.

Then the second decision has to be made to which LTP archive this data set should be sent, the humanities, social sciences or the technical sciences, except biomedical. In the Dutch situation humanities and social sciences are sent to DANS. The technical data sets are sent to the 3TU Data Centre. Using only the metadata fields currently available in the ORE descriptors, it is difficult to determine fully reliably the target LTP archive. The origin of the EP institutional repository (EP-IR) might give some indication for this science split.

Origin of Publication

Another complicating factor is that some LTP archives may enforce restrictions on the acceptable content, such as only publications from its own country. Publications originating in other countries have to be preserved elsewhere. Again the current set of minimal metadata per EP component does not allow for automatic decisions here. This problem could not be solved in this LTP demonstrator.

Persistent Identifiers

As described in Paragraph 19.3, in the current Dutch LTP procedure a publication is harvested by the KB and at a later instance in the process the DIAS assigns an internal identifier when the item is ingested in the e-Depot. In EPs there is a separate resource descriptor with a reference (URI) to the content. When stored in distributed LTP archives, these references point to the original objects in the IRs but not to the related parts of the EP in the other LTP archives. If references become invalid they should be changed into the newly created identifiers. This problem will not be solved in this demonstrator.

Preservation Problems

Another complicating factor is that it is not always clear which LTP archive has the preservation responsibility for some EP components. An appropriate LTP archive may even not exist at the processing time of the EP preservation. It has to be decided how to handle such cases. This is more an organisational than a technical issue. A full preservation of the EP is not possible in such cases. The EP management of the Institutional Repository should be warned that long-term preservation has only been partially successful in this case.

20.4 Considerations

The proposed solution has advantages and disadvantages. We list a few of them here.

Access Restrictions

Due to access restrictions to items in other IRs, it may be not allowed for the EP-Transformer to obtain a copy of an EP component. In such a case only the Persistant Identifier can be included in the container with the resolved results. All responsibility for long-term availability then remains at the original repository. The EP-Transformer can only be fully operational if the EP and all its components have 'open access' rights.

Infinite Recursion

A resource graph with its dependency relations may contain cycles leading to infinite resolving activity. Proper and carefully designed algorithms inside the EP-Transformer might be able to deal with this issue. The same goes for other errors in graphs like missing links. The archiving agreement should show which partner is responsible and how the other should react.

Duplicates

Different EPs can aggregate the same component. The resolving mechanism envisioned here does not take this into account. It leads to duplicates of the component in the LTP archive. For the demo this is certainly not a problem, but for large-scale use later on this issue should be resolved. Keeping track of which items are already in the LTP archive is one possibility. Or one could argue that this kind of redundancy has to be accepted in a 'fragmented world'. Persistent identifiers only solve this issue to a certain level.

Changing EPs

The EP structure and components may change over time. Keeping track of these changes dynamically is a very ambitious goal. For the time being we consider taking snapshots at regular intervals within the lifetime of an EP, until nobody changes it anymore, as a sufficient approach. Putting the responsibility at the EP-IRs may be a solution for this issue. When the EP-IR offers a new version of the EP ready for harvesting, it will be preserved. Each time this happens, a complete new EP with all its components is preserved[114].

A consequence of the decision to make the aggregation document part of all archives involved is that, if an EP is edited or expanded with new resources, the aggregation document in the different archives could become inconsistent, due to different time schemes or harvest policies. A push mechanism on the site of the EP-IR makes the IR exclusively responsible for updating all the connected archives.

Institutional Responsibilities

Considering all of this, there are the following three roles: the IR role, the LTP archiving role and the EP transformer role. In the future the EP-Transformer role can be included in the IR or on the LTP archive side or its actions can be split among different parties. The EP-Transformer functionality will remain the same. In this demonstrator we have

---

[114] See Paragraph 19.3

developed the EP-Transformer as a separate entity for ease of development. In the future and after proper adaptation such a service could be incorporated into the KB infrastructure. We have designed the EP-Transformer in a way that alleviates the barriers for such a step.

20.5   Conclusion

The LTP demonstrator shows at which aspects the current infrastructure should be expanded, based on the Dutch situation. We developed a mechanism that takes the aggregation document and makes containers for ePrints as well as research data sets. As there is currently no institution taking care of the long-term preservation of the document that describes the structure of the EP, the decision was made to include the whole aggregation document in both containers. The consequence is that if an EP is edited or expanded with new resources, the aggregation document in the different archives could become inconsistent, due to different time schemes or harvest policies. The main issue for preserving the relations between the parts of an EP in whatever situation is the assignment and maintenance of persistent identifiers to parts of EP's. ePrints and research data could wander from one repository to another and are duplicated, in some cases as the only remaining copy, in LTP archives. Still, over time, the resource map holds identifiers that point to a specific place on the Internet and the identifiers should somehow be resolved to find the actual place were the resource is held.

21. Archiving Agreement and Enhanced Publications

21.1 Introduction

This chapter will discuss the different aspects of an archiving agreement for EPs. An outline is given for an agreement that can be used as the basis for a real agreement.

Archiving is a difficult task with multiple stakeholders, responsibilities and uncertainties. Archiving an EP is even more complex, because it involves components of different types with in the most complex case different owners. An archiving agreement is essential to identify the stakeholders and responsibilities and define who is responsible for what and to what extent.

A few assumptions are made in order to get grip on the problem of archiving EPs. The first assumption is that a repository acts on behalf of the originator of a component, thus having a license to deposit. The second assumption is that, in case the components of the EP's need to be stored in separate LTP archives, there is a procedure that determines for every component by which LTP archive it will be stored.

A note on this last remark might be helpful. Although in general all components of an EP will be stored in one LTP archive, the topic of the demonstrator is the Dutch situation, where the components might be spread over several LTP archives, dependent of the kind of object. This will highly influence the complexity of the archiving agreements. This is probably not the most usual situation.

21.2 Identification of Stakeholders

This paragraph explores all the relevant stakeholders, objects and responsibilities with regard to the long-term preservation of an EP. An EP is archived when all of its individual components are archived:
- Individual components;
- Metadata of components;
- Relations;
- Metadata of relations.

The following actors are involved in archiving EPs:
- Data Producer[115];
- LTP archives.

Figure 28 gives an overview of the Data Producer on the left, the components of an EP in the middle, and the LTP archives on the right.

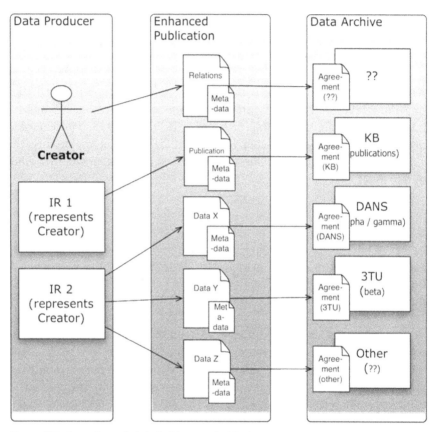

Figure 28. Overview of stakeholders and objects

At this time, it is unclear when an EP will be archived. For the sake of simplicity we make the following assumptions:
- The data producer initiates sending the EP or its components to the LTP archive. The data producer can be the researcher him/herself or an institutional repository representing the researcher. Archiving starts with the resource map. This defines the components of an EP.

---

[115] Because we state that an IR acts on behalf of the creator, also has a licence tot deposit, the data producer is the IR.

There should be a check for each component whether it is already archived or whether it still needs to be archived. If all components are archived then the relations can be archived;
- Each component is a autonomous entity and has no dependency of parts in another archives;
- The resource map in the EP will show the LTP archive if components of the EP are stored in other archives;
- The archives are assumed to be capable of archiving and preserving the components of the EPs;
- The relations are to be preserved by using persistent identifiers;
- Each relation usually consists of an object, a relation-type and a target, e.g. document doc1 references dataset dat2. The use of persistent identifiers divides archiving relations into two responsibilities, the permanent storage of the triple object-relation-target and the commitment to maintain the current location with the persistent identifiers.

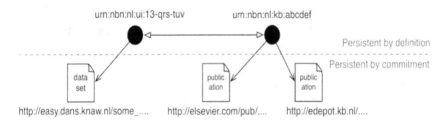

Figure 29. Preserving Relations

Figure 29 shows how the relation between the objects *urn:nbn:nl:ui-13-qrs-tuv* and *urn:nbn:nl:kb:abcdef* is persistent by definition. None of these identifiers have to change over time. The relation between these identifiers and the current location is not necessarily persistent. The locations of these objects may change. Commitment from the repositories or archives is needed to update these relations when this happens.

21.3 Issues that have to be addressed in an Agreement

21.3.1 Archiving Agreements in general
As shown above, parts of an EP will be archived in a long-term archive. The objects these archives will store might differ in appearance, depending on the specific part of the EP, and may range for example from websites to data, and from ePrints to music. Apart from storing the EPs,

the LTP archives will store other material as well as a consequence of its scope and mission and so deal with other suppliers (Producers) of digital material.

In most cases the LTP archives will already have archiving agreements with the producers of the digital material they archive. In some cases this will be on a legal basis, e.g. national libraries with deposit laws in different countries. Sometimes this is extended with specific require-ments. All these archiving agreements will deal with aspects like responsibilities, material that will be delivered, and access rights. They will be inspired by rules and regulations as formulated in the OAIS model, TRAC, the DANS Data Seal of Approval, and the archives experi-ences. Most of this information will be rather static and on a high level.

For day to day operations there is often a separate part in the archiving agreement, sometimes called 'work procedures' in which the LTP archives have described in more detail the day to day activities, like the description of the SIP, the metadata, the delivery scheme and amount of objects, and contact persons. These work procedures of the agree-ment will be evaluated regularly and updated when necessary.

Not all material that LTP archives store has an owner that can be iden-tified, take for example websites, and without an owner it will not be possible to have an archiving agreement.

For the long-term preservation of EPs, both the archiving agreement and the work procedures of the archiving agreement need to be adapted. On a general level, the LTP archive will describe its intentions. On a detailed level, these intentions will be translated into practical approaches.

21.3.2 Enhanced Publications and Archiving Agreements

Preservation Policies

One of the characteristics of EPs in relation to LTP archives is that dif-ferent parts of the EP may be stored in different LTP archives. As EP's may also be stored in one LTP archive this will not always be the case, but in this study we focus on the most complex situation.

In case the components are distributed over different LTP archives, an issue raises regarding preservation policies. Each LTP archive will have developed its own preservation policies. This could lead to different approaches in handling long-term preservation of the parts of the EPs if the LTP archives do not synchronise their approaches towards the preservation of these EPs. This synchronisation will be a permanent activity, as there must be a constant alignment of policies between archives. The question is whether this is realistic to assume. But if this synchronisation does not happen, there will be a risk for the preservation of the EP. Preservation of EPs is more than archiving the individual parts of it.

In order to realise this, the LTP archives should reach a mutual approach on certain aspects:
• Starting points with regard to the material;
• Persistent Identifier(s);
• Usability and Access.

Starting Points with Regard to the Material
• *File Formats.* The LTP archive must have sufficient control over the content. This is not specific for EPs. For research information parts of the EP might be created with dedicated software of which no publicly available information exists. This is certainly a risk for preservation. The LTP archive may handle this in different ways. It could either not accept this material as a consequence of its policy, or indicate that it cannot take full responsibility for the preservation of the EP by using a preservation level, or it could migrate the material to a more acceptable file format, or it agrees with the producer that it will receive all relevant information for preservation. Policies about which file formats will be accepted under which conditions should be part of the archiving agreement and the archives involved should harmonise their approach.

• *Preservation and other Rights.* In order to get full control of the parts of the EP, the archives involved need to be sure that it has the necessary copyrights and legal permission to do so, because in case one of the components of the EP has insufficient rights, this might affect the preservation of the whole EP. If, for example, there is no permission to perform preservation activities on one of the component, this component might not be accessible in the future and thus the EP will be incomplete. This implies that the original producer, whether repository or researcher, should safeguard the LTP archive against claims of other parties. It might also be possible that some rights will not be solved, and that parts of the EP might not be accessed.

- *User Community.* In order to preserve the digital material faithfully, the intended audience that will access the EP material, in OAIS terminology the Designated Community, should be known. In the case of research information the material will be created in different communities, each with their own characteristics and standards. The future user should have knowledge about these community-specific aspects that are necessary to understand the digital objects from this community fully. Therefore this information should be preserved too. The archiving agreement could contain a description of this audience and the specific measures taken to serve this audience. The archives involved should harmonise their view on the intended designated community in their archiving agreements.

- *Authenticity.* As parts of the EP may originate from different repositories, and may have moved in the past from place to place, it is not only important to update the persistent identifier resolvers, but also to convince the user about the authenticity of the parts of the EP. How the authenticity will be proved, will be described in the archiving agreement, e.g. which metadata on provenance or significant properties will be added to the components.

- *Status of the Enhanced Publication Part.* The LTP archive needs to be sure that the part of the EP that it will store is an autonomous entity and has a certain degree of readiness for long-term preservation. It makes no sense to archive unfinished ePrints or datasets that will be updated on a regular basis unless this is part of the way the EP is archived, e.g. by making snapshots of the component. This is a similar approach as taken by the LTP archive with websites. The components of the EP need to have a status that supports the moment of LTP archiving. The data producer needs to be aware of this. The repository should enforce it, so that the LTP archive can assume this at the moment of accepting the content of an EP. The archiving agreement will describe under which conditions an EP will be accepted. In case several archives are involved, they will have to harmonise their conditions.

Persistent Identifier(s)

Persistent identifiers relate the various parts of the EP to each other. Losing these identifiers means losing the extra value of the EP. So each LTP archive that stores part of the EP should take appropriate measures to maintain these persistent identifiers. When an LTP archive sends its material to another archive, this change of location should be updated in the resolver.

One thing an archiving agreement between an LTP and an IR is not able to solve, is the question of who will maintain the resolver for the long term. This vital link in the chain will have an owner and it with this organisation that the LTP archive should make an agreement.

Usability and Access
A minimum set of bibliographic metadata must be included in the EP that the LTP archive will store, to enable the LTP archive to make the EP accessible, persistent identifiers being a part of this.

21.3.3   Preservation Actions
Each LTP archive will have its own strategies for preservation actions in case an object is at risk. These preservation actions might influence the usability and accessibility of the part of the EP in the archive and so the total EP. The archiving agreement should be clear about this. And, in case more than one LTP archive is involved, these actions should be well coordinated.

21.4   Extra Agreements

So far on the archiving agreement and work procedures. In many cases, one could imagine that there is also a Service Level Agreement, in which issues like response time and service time is regulated. However, these agreements will be made up between each archive and its service provider or IT department and are beyond scope here.

21.5   Conclusion

According to Van Godtsenhoven (2009) preservation of an EP is not only a technical issue, but also an important organisational issue[116]. In this chapter the distinctive organisational roles that play part in the long-term preservation of EP are described. Based upon this, we give suggestions for aspects that should be included in an archiving agreement. The actual content of each agreement, however, could be

---

[116] See Paragraph 4.6 in: Godsenhoven, Karin van (ed.) Emerging Standards for Enhanced Publications and Repository Technology. SURFfoundation, 2009

different from country to country, due to legal regulations or national organisation. Apart from the archiving agreement between an IR and a LTP archive, attention should be given to the long-term preservation of the resolver as this resolver contains the vital information to realise the recreation of a complete EP.

22. General Conclusions

After an overview of the main issues in long-term archiving of digital publications, we described the connection between the Dutch university IRs and the long-term preservation facility in the National Library of the Netherlands (KB). A demonstrator was created to show where the current infrastructure should be expanded based on the Dutch situation and to detect some issues that need further research and discussion. Although the LTP situation in the Netherlands is specific, with different archives for different type of resources, this situation of working with several archives for archiving one EP is realistic. The different resources could originate from different countries and different institutions. It might be an illusion that the world-width research community will come to one consistent regulation for EPs. Above that, parts of the EP will be archived already in more than one LTP archive.

The conclusion is that the persistent identifier infrastructure is essential for preserving an EP. In national or international regulations of long-term preservation special attention should be paid to the preservation of the resolvers as an essential part of a persistent long-term preservation infrastructure for EPs. Working with mirror sites and pushing the persistent identifier properties to each other by comparing the DNS structure of the IP-addresses on internet could be a possibility, but is not completely according to LTP standards.

LTP archives should have a preservation policy in which they describe which preservation actions they will undertake in case risks are identified that might affect their archived digital objects. As for EPs, tuning the preservation policies of the different LTP archives that take care of parts of the EP and have a shared responsibility is even more important, as different approaches might lead to inaccessible EPs and loss of authenticity.

Issues that need further research and discussion are the following:
- The data provider is responsible for the consistency of an EP and for the archiving act of an EP. To this, there must be a reliable infrastructure for persistent identifiers in all countries involved in archiving parts of the EP.

- Resolvers are essential in a persistent identifier infrastructure. Further discussion is needed about the long-term preservation aspects of resolvers.
- Parts of EPs will be often archived in different archives. The party responsible for the EP must have sufficient means to declare what the nature is of the different parts of the EP and where the different parts should be archived, based on archiving agreements. These properties must be captured in standardised metadata fields with a standardised vocabulary.
- In case an EP is split up in different parts for being archived in different places, it is necessary to store the whole research map together with all the parts of the EP. When starting to access an EP from one of the archives involved, one will have sufficient information in this resource map to retrieve the other parts of the EP. The liability of the links in the resource map depends on the liability of the persistent identifier infrastructure.
- It may not be allowed for the archives involved to obtain together a copy of all EP components, due to access restrictions to items in other IRs. In such a case only the permanent identifier in the resource map can be included. All responsibility for long-term availability of not archived parts of the EP then remains at the original repository.
- Different EPs can aggregate the same component. It could lead to duplicates of the component in the LTP archive. Keeping track of which items are already in the LTP archive is one possibility to deal with duplicates. Persistent and unique identifiers could add to the solution of this issue, but only in the situation where just one archive is involved.
- The EP structure and components may change over time. Keeping track of these changes dynamically is a very ambitious goal. For the time being we consider taking snapshots at regular intervals within the lifetime, until nobody changes it anymore, of an EP as a sufficient solution. It is the data producers responsibility to offer a new version of the EP for archiving. Each time this happens, a complete new EP with all its components is preserved, unless a data producer indicates sufficiently which parts of the EP are changed and the archive has the mechanism to deal with versions.
- A consequence of the decision to include the complete aggregation document in the different SIPs with the different parts of an EP is that if an EP is edited or expanded with new resources, there could arise inconsistency between the aggregation documents in the

different archives, due to different time schemes or harvest policies. The responsible IR should push the updates to all archives involved.

- Storing the complete resource map in every place where a part of an EP is archived make the archives less dependent from each other. As this will cause a risk for the integrity of the references, a possible better solution could be to establish a separate instance for archiving the resource maps of EPs and to extend the resolving infrastructure of persistent identifiers with an automated updating mechanism for archived documents, regardless if these documents are part of an EP. The archiving party could be the same as one of the archives for object parts of the EP. Adequate agreements between the archives responsible for archiving the resource map and the other parties are essential.

Appendix. Work Agreements

This version of Work Agreements between Koninklijke Bibliotheek and an Institutional Repository is a draft (April 2009) made to add a new group of IRs to the network. Every agreement is edited according to the situation of the specific IR or group of IRs. Those specific remarks are skipped as well as the name of the party.

Introduction

The e-Depot is a digital archive environment for permanent access to digital information sources. Without this environment, digital sources would become unreadable at a rapid pace, because software and hardware quickly become obsolete and the information carriers have a limited lifespan. The aim of the e-Depot is thus to store the Depot of Dutch Electronic Publications (DNEP), and secure permanent access to scientific information for the research community. The e-Depot's core, the Digital Information Archiving System (DIAS), is based on the OAIS reference model, an international standard. The Koninklijke Bibliotheek (National Library of the Netherlands hereafter referred to as the KB) uses transparent procedures for including and processing digital publications.

Quality control is part of its inclusion policy as well as the actual processing of e-Depot objects. The e-Depot has been developed to facilitate permanent storage and long-term access; migration and emulation procedures are being developed as strategies for permanent access. Fully integrated into its organisation, long-term archiving of digital publications is part of the KB's collection policy and daily processing processes. Its Research and Development department continuously studies new developments in digital sustainability in an international context. The e-Depot system and the quality of the processing processes for digital publications are regularly updated, and new tools are also developed and implemented for this purpose. The KB strives for international certification of the e-Depot to reflect its quality.

Within the context of the DARE[117] project, and for the purpose of long-term storage and permanent access to the digital objects[118] of Dutch

---

[117] See also www.narcis.info/index/tab/darenet/

Institutional Repositories (IRs), a link has been established between these IRs and the KB's e-Depot. This will enable the IRs to use services made available by the KB for long-term storage of digital publications. This means that the IRs need not invest in this themselves.

In its e-Depot, the KB will ensure sustainable archiving of the publications collected [...]. To this end, these work agreements have been formulated, which are based on the following general principles:

1. the work agreements entered into with the IRs within the framework of Digital Academic Repositories (DARE);
2. the general policy on the sustainable archiving of publications set out in the archiving agreements entered into with publishers within the context of the international e-Depot;
3. the KB's ability, for the time being, to ensure only the sustainable archiving of text files; therefore, datasets will not be part of these work agreements;
4. the KB's general policy that publications archived in the e-Depot be accessible on site for KB-registered users, in line with agreements with publishers;
5. the idea that [...] project will pay a limited fee for the initial costs of setting up this service and the storage of [...] publications.

1   Depositing and archiving

1.1   The KB will only include publications offered open accessible by IRs. The IRs are individually responsible for formal coordination with authors regarding the publications offered in the repositories for harvesting.

1.2   The objects will only be included in the e-Depot if they are available in one of the agreed file formats and their metadata satisfy the DAREnet guidelines (see also 3). Appendix A contains a list of permitted formats [note: omitted]. This list may be updated during the period of these work agreements.

1.3   From the perspective of sustainability, non-proprietary or general and common formats are preferred. At least once a year, [...] and the KB will consult on the accepted file formats.

---

[118] In this context, 'objects is defined by DARE as "... those objects that are made available on the public Internet through the IRs. A copy of those objects will enter the e-Depot of the Koninklijke Bibliotheek." In: *"Report DARE – Specifications for a Networked Repository", version 3.0, August 2003, section 4.3.3. "Requirements of the DARE partners relating to archiving and preservation"*

1.4 The KB will convert text files harvested from the IRs other than in PDF format to PDF-A, but will always save the original file in the original format along with the converted version.

1.5 The KB will aim for permanent sustainable access of digital objects. For this reason, it will only harvest and include metadata with corresponding objects in the e-Depot. When a metadata file does not include an external reference to an object, the KB will assume that there is no corresponding object and the relevant record does not require harvesting.

1.6 The KB will permanently include the objects in the e-Depot and not remove archived objects. It will ignore so-called "deletes" from the OAI protocol, but can restrict access to them at the request of the relevant IR (see also 5.3).

1.7 The IRs will enable the KB to harvest objects monthly. A fixed contact person within [...] will make the data available to the KB which are needed for the harvesting process (i.e. the URLs of the repositories to be harvested and the corresponding set names). The KB will harvest each IR at a set time as far as possible. [...] will inform the KB when harvesting is impossible for various reasons.

1.8 An object may be included in various IRs (for example when several university researchers work together on a publication). This 'doubling' is also possible (or perhaps inevitable) when harvesting the same objects in the e-Depot or within the framework of DAREnet. To prevent the doubling of Dutch repositories in the e-Depot, the [...] contact person will not supply the KB with the data of these repositories, or will indicate that they need not be harvested.

2 Metadata

2.1 [...]

2.2 The KB must be informed of any changes to the metadata structure as early as possible to be able to make timely adjustments to its own processes. All changes must be forwarded to the KB via a single [...] contact.

2.3 The KB will inform [...] of any deviations it observes in the metadata compared to the guidelines. To this end, the KB will conduct a once-only quality control before starting the harvesting process. Any necessary adjustments will be made, followed by a new quality control. In the event of deviations, the KB is authorised not to include the objects until the situation is resolved.

2.4 In line with the general e-Depot policy, the KB will include metadata of the archived IR objects in the KB catalogue. To this end, it will convert the metadata supplied by the IRs into its own metadata structure.

3 Sustainable storage and permanent access

3.1 To be able to optimally store the objects from the IRs and ensure access to them, the KB will carry out continuous research into all relevant aspects. It will also commit itself to performing preservation actions when needed to secure access to the objects. As a precondition for this, IRs will offer files in line with the list of permitted file formats.

3.2 The KB will keep [...] informed of the procedures for the actions needed to keep deposited objects accessible.

4 Findability and return of objects

4.1 The KB does not intend to offer special services using the objects harvested from the IRs, such as providing separate access to these objects or a separate entry in the KB catalogue.

4.2 The metadata of the IR-harvested objects can be consulted via the KB catalogue. [...]

4.3 If it has serious reason to do so, the IR can request that the KB make certain IR objects no longer freely accessible. The KB assumes that the IRs have implemented procedures for "notice and take down". Publications removed from an IR as a result of this procedure will no longer be shown via the e-Depot at the specific request of the IRs.

4.4 The KB will not harvest embargoed content. However, the IRs must individually ensure that embargoed content does not end up in the set to be harvested by the KB.

4.5 [...] can request that the KB return the objects of a specific IR. This can happen per batch, selected on the basis of a date indicated by the individual IR in the metadata (using the elements <date> and <dateModified>) and/or file format and format version.

4.6 If the IR has supplied multiple versions of the same objects, the most recent version will be returned. Older versions will, naturally, be stored. As a precondition for the KB to be able return the latest version, the harvester must be able to identify that version. This is only possible when the IRs make careful use of the date field in the metadata (DateModified).

4.7   [...] will submit a request by email to the KB's e-Depot department (E-depot.mailbox@kb.nl) if it wishes to have objects returned. The KB will post the requested objects within three weeks of receiving the request on the KB's FTP server. Objects will be returned free of charge.

5   Other agreements
5.1   To be able to respond adequately to changes at the IRs and to optimise the harvesting process, it is important to inform the KB of changes in good time. These may include changes to the metadata at element level, repository name, basic URL, metadata prefix, set name and setspec, and the IR administrator's contact details.
5.2   Changes to the e-Depot must be forwarded in good time to the IRs.
5.3   [...]

6   Duration of the work agreements
6.1   These work agreements will take effect on [...] and will be evaluated and preferably set down in a contract by the end [...]. This does not apply to the list of permitted file formats, which will be adjusted when needed.

7   Costs
7.1   [...]
7.2   The cooperation between [...] and the KB, including its financial aspects, will be evaluated by the end of [...].

For Product Safety Concerns and Information please contact our EU
representative GPSR@taylorandfrancis.com
Taylor & Francis Verlag GmbH, Kaufingerstraße 24, 80331 München, Germany